AF173977

"This book is a keeper, and one you will refer to over and over again."
—LYNN CONNERY, READING RECOVERY TEACHER LEADER

"Each chapter of *Welcome to Reading Workshop: Structures and Routines that Support All Readers* provides a practical guide to implementing reading workshop through building community, powerful minilessons, interactive read-alouds, explicit instruction, authentic classroom-based assessments, and the value of independent reading."
—JESSICA KILCOLLUM, READING SPECIALIST, GRADES 3–5

"No matter what curriculum you teach or how long you have taught, this book is filled with practical ideas to lift student voices and allow them to take charge of their learning process."
—TAMMY MULLIGAN, SECOND-GRADE TEACHER AND AUTHOR

"This book is a valuable resource for educators of all experience levels."
—DR. JEN GREENE, SECOND-GRADE TEACHER

"How Lynne and Brenda break down complicated, multifaceted strategies into educator-friendly, and more importantly, child-friendly approaches, is refreshing and effective for any classroom."
—PETER CATALANOTTO, CHILDREN'S BOOK AUTHOR AND ILLUSTRATOR

"This book is the most comprehensive I have read on this topic and will provide any teacher with everything they need to support diverse readers in their classrooms!"
—DR. PEGGY HICKMAN, ASSOCIATE PROFESSOR OF EDUCATION, ARCADIA UNIVERSITY

"Centering on sustaining literacy communities, the chapters provide timely resources to infuse the reading workshop framework within today's busy classrooms. *Welcome to Reading Workshop* gives educators the tools to build a community of readers, leverage culturally relevant read-alouds, model explicit instruction through minilessons, and support professional collaboration. The inclusion of video clips, book recommendations, minilesson templates, photographs, and reflection questions make this an accessible and purpose-driven resource for educators, administrators, and all who care deeply about building students' capacity as readers."

—Dr. Mary Napoli, Associate Professor of Reading,
School of Behavioral Sciences and Education

"Lynne and Brenda have written a practical guide for teachers, new and seasoned, to assist in developing a strong and sound reading workshop in their classrooms."

—Emily Reed, Reading Specialist

"*Welcome to Reading Workshop* is a treasure chest of goodies for all teachers to launch and maintain a healthy reading workshop all year long. But the deep groove of this book is the vibe of togetherness and humanity—the real magic of a reading workshop."

—Gaetan Pappalardo, Third-Grade Teacher

"*Welcome to Reading Workshop* is a one stop shop for reading workshop. Written for first year teachers and veteran teachers alike, this book includes all the essential components that is needed to run an effective reading workshop."

—Dr. Beverly Hanrahan, Reading Specialist,
Certified Reading Recovery Teacher

"Lynne Dorfman and Brenda Krupp present teachers with real class scenarios, along with a lesson format that includes engaging book talks, choice clubs, and meaningful responses to inspire young minds on fire!"

—Eileen T. Hutchinson, WCASD, Reading Specialist,
PA Writing and Literature Fellow 99'/05'

"Brenda Krupp and Lynne Dorfman offer tried and true suggestions, anticipating and answering questions and concerns for novices and veterans alike. *Welcome to Reading Workshop* should be on every teacher's bookshelf!"

—Judith Jester, Curriculum Supervisor
for Language Arts & Social Studies

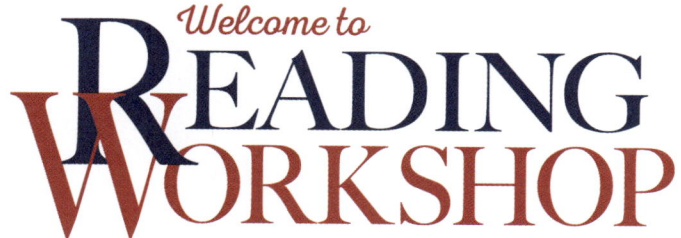

Welcome to

READING
WORKSHOP

STRUCTURES AND ROUTINES THAT SUPPORT ALL READERS

BRENDA J. KRUPP & LYNNE R. DORFMAN

Foreword by Laura Robb

www.stenhouse.com

Copyright © 2023 by Brenda J. Krupp and Lynne R. Dorfman

All rights reserved. Except for pages in the appendix, which can be photocopied for classroom use, no part of this publication may be reproduced or transmitted in any form or by any means, electronic or mechanical, including photocopy, or any information storage and retrieval system, without permission from the publisher.

Every effort has been made to contact copyright holders and students for permission to reproduce borrowed material. We regret any oversights that may have occurred and will be pleased to rectify them in subsequent reprints of the work.

Figure 3.3, Copyright © 2002 by Jim Arnosky. All rights reserved.

Figure 3.6, From *Million Dollar Shot* by Dan Gutman, copyright © 1997. Reprinted by permission of Little, Brown Books for Young Readers, an imprint of Hachette Book Group, Inc.

Figure 6.1a, From *Every Soul a Star* by Wendy Mass, copyright © 2008. Reprinted by permission of Little Brown Books for Young Readers, an imprint of Hachette Book Group, Inc.

Figure 6.1a, *Dreamland* by Sarah Dessen.© 2004. Used by permission of Penguin Random House.

Figure 6.1d, *Circus Mirandus* by Cassie Beasley. © 2015. Used by permission of Penguin Random House.

Figure 6.1d, From *Mousenet* by Prudence Breitrose, copyright © 2013. Reprinted by permission of Little, Brown Young Readers Plus, an imprint of Hachette Book Group, Inc.

Figure 6.2, From *The Magic School Bus Inside a Hurricane* by Joanna Cole, illustrated by Bruce Degen. Text copyright © 1996 by Joanna Cole. Illustrations copyright © 1996 by Bruce Degen. Reprinted by permission of Scholastic Inc.

Figure 8.4, *Bully Trouble* by Joanna Cole. © 1989. Used by permission of Penguin Random House.

Figure 9.3, *Next Year in Havana* by Chanel Cleeton. © 2018. Used by permission of Penguin Random House.

Library of Congress Cataloging-in-Publication Data

Names: Dorfman, Lynne R., 1952- author. | Krupp, Brenda J., author.
Title: Welcome to reading workshop : structures and routines that support all readers / Brenda J. Krupp and Lynne R. Dorfman.
Description: Portsmouth, New Hampshire: Stenhouse Publishers, [2023] | Includes bibliographical references and index. |
Identifiers: LCCN 2023006379 (print) | LCCN 2023006380 (ebook) | ISBN 9781625315304 (paperback : alk. paper) | ISBN 9781625315311 (ebook)
Subjects: LCSH: Reading. | Reading comprehension–Study and teaching. | Children–Books and reading. | Classroom libraries. | Effective teaching.
Classification: LCC LB1050.45 .D67 2023 (print) | LCC LB1050.45 (ebook) | DDC 372.4–dc23/eng/20230411
LC record available at https://lccn.loc.gov/2023006379
LC ebook record available at https://lccn.loc.gov/2023006380

Cover design, interior design, and typesetting by Page2, LLC.

Printed in the United States of America

This book is printed on paper certified by third-party standards for sustainably managed foresty.

29 28 27 26 25 24 23   11335   9 8 7 6 5 4 3 2 1

FROM BRENDA

For my dad, Tom Telford, who shared his love of reading with me when I was a child, and still does. *Thanks, Dad!*

FROM LYNNE

For Alex, Brooke, and Caitlyn, my wonderful goddaughters, who bring love, laughter, and sunshine into my life.

Contents

Video Table of Contents

CHAPTER 7

CHAPTER 8

CHAPTER 9

CHAPTER 10

Foreword

When I listen to an orchestra, I marvel at how the conductor pulls together four separate sections—strings, brass, woodwind, and percussion—to perform a symphony. Their music takes me on an emotional journey that illustrates the power of four distinct orchestra parts blending together to create a symphony of sounds that affects me deeply. I'm lost in the music, and time stops.

This is how I felt when I read *Welcome to Reading Workshop* by Brenda Krupp and Lynne Dorfman. They took me on a reading workshop journey that, like an orchestra, has many complex parts working together to develop students' passion for reading now and for a lifetime!

As an author, teacher, and international speaker, I presently coach teachers and find that it can be a challenge to help new and less experienced teachers as well as traditional teachers risk embracing reading workshop. While reading *Welcome to Reading Workshop*, I felt as if the authors were speaking directly to me, providing answers to the four questions teachers repeatedly ask about reading workshop: *Can I still include my district's phonics requirements? Can I fit in the required grade level anthology? How can I organize and manage flexible grouping? How do I know my students are really reading books they choose?* Brenda and Lynne show that none of these questions are impediments to organizing a reading workshop when they write, "In addition to its ability to efficiently address literacy standards and meet the varied needs of the learners in your reading community, the workshop approach encourages flexibility based on the direct needs of both. The familiar structure and key components of a reading workshop fit seamlessly into any language arts block" (page 10). Explicit phonics instruction fits into reading workshop and occurs during a minilesson followed by guided practice, by using flexible grouping when teachers pull small groups of students to work on specific skills and strategies they need to practice, and by holding one-on-one and/or small group conferences. Required district anthologies, the authors point out, are an excellent resource during reading workshop because the themes and genres introduced can be used to extend book clubs and literature circles. Conferences, students' written responses, book talks, and small group shares all reveal students' recall and comprehension of books they're reading. When the authors address specific district requirements and show how they can enhance students' reading growth, they develop a flexible and powerful workshop model.

Fundamental to the strength of this book is the variety of ways Brenda and Lynne increase teachers' understanding of the elements of reading workshop. I love that they included at least one video in each of the ten chapters. Videos invite you to observe a procedural minilesson (you'll find plans for this lesson in **Appendix D**), listen as poet Janet Wong recounts a childhood story that highlights how children identify themselves and connect with books, watch an assistant superintendent discuss the value of independent reading, or observe how children reflect on their reading work and set goals during share time. Not only do these videos breathe authenticity into reading workshop topics, but they also offer you the option of re-watching them again and again to enlarge your mental model of reading workshop's routines and rituals. Also threaded through each chapter are teacher tips, sample anchor charts, captioned photographs, and a contribution feature that, in brief paragraphs, offers different teachers' takes on "What is reading workshop?" Chapters close with two features that encourage reflection and action. The first invites you to use questions in "Stop and Reflect" to make connections to the content as well as examine personal experiences related to the information. The second, "Something to Try," asks you to implement an idea in the chapter, such as keeping a reader's notebook for your own reading in order to better understand the work students are doing.

Like the parts of an orchestra, these repeated features work together, helping you visualize the interplay of the diverse elements of a reading workshop. Built on the solid foundation of current and established research in reading, the authors also include literacy snapshots from elementary school teachers and students. By adding layers of authentic stories about reading workshop, the authors provide a supportive network for teachers

and coaches, developing deep and lasting connections to the information in each chapter.

I have written about reading workshop for middle school and have read many books about it for all grades. But this gem of a book is my pick for elementary school teachers because every chapter is a reminder to teach the children in front of you, to differentiate lessons, to develop students' reading identities, and to lead each child into the reading life. As Brenda and Lynne shine the spotlight on one reading workshop element at a time, they bring clarity to how each part strengthens teaching and supports students' learning and reading progress.

Throughout *Welcome to Reading Workshop* the authors show that choice belongs to students and teachers and builds agency for both groups. Since the learning needs of teachers and students differ and continually grow and change as the school year unfolds, Brenda and Lynne include robust choice lists in chapters, allowing both groups to select suggestions that benefit their evolving needs. They ask you to learn from and with your students to refine how to create a community of readers, use daily read-alouds, guided reading, small group work, minilessons, conferring, formative assessments, and culturally relevant classroom libraries. They ask you to be learners who grow and change by kidwatching and reading and discussing professional books and articles. They ask you to remain focused on the book's overarching purpose: to develop joyful, lifelong readers.

The subtitle of the *Welcome to Reading Workshop*'s introduction sums up the goal of this book: "A Model to Help Students Become Readers." Brenda and Lynne remind you that every student in your classes deserves opportunities to improve their reading skill and then experience the joy of getting lost in a book that they select. In a workshop, when reading joy combines with responsive teaching, both of them nurture children's love of reading. This can best happen with *Welcome to Reading Workshop* by your side, guiding you through the process while helping every child develop a lifelong passion for reading.

– *Laura Robb*

Acknowledgments

Over the years, we have been fortunate to work with many wonderful students, teachers, and administrators. We've attended conferences including NCTE, ILA, PCTELA, and KSLA as presenters and participants. Those professional organizations, along with our work with the West Chester Writing Project (Pennsylvania Writing & Literature Project), have provided a network of teachers K–12 and beyond with whom to share ideas and imagine the possibilities. Our experiences have led us to writing this book.

We started to think about this book two years ago. We met at a Wegmans food market for coffee and talked about what would be most helpful to preservice and novice teachers in the literacy domain. *Welcome to Writing Workshop* had been published in 2019, and we searched the professional books for a similar book that addressed components of a reading workshop. Of course, we found many incredible books that helped to guide our decisions, but none that looked like the book we wanted to write. The authors of these books have been our mentors for a long time— Regie Routman, Lucy Calkins, Richard Allington, Laura Robb, Debbie Miller, Stephanie Harvey, and Ann Goudvis. Over the last two decades we found new mentors too, reading the work of Donalyn Miller, Kelly Gallagher, Colby Sharp, Rita Bean, Sonja Cherry-Paul, Jennifer Allen, Terry Thompson, Ernest Morrell, and Pam Allyn. We collected a small mountain of books and articles, reading and rereading to create an outline that would scaffold our thinking and writing. We are grateful for their passion and commitment to the teaching profession and the work they have shared with us to help teachers create communities of readers.

Then we visited classrooms. Brenda's third graders helped us think about everything that a reading workshop is made of. Other teachers at Franconia Elementary in Souderton Area School District welcomed us into their rooms. A big thank you to Theresa Hunsicker, Kim Harsanyi, and

Tammi Lelii. We were able to watch and tape a procedural minilesson in Theresa's first grade class and observe independent reading time, including partner reading. In fifth grade, students mapped their readerly lives, gathered in book clubs to discuss books, and, every so often, self-monitored their reading fluency by recording their reading rates with a stopwatch. Thank you, Dr. Laura Heineck, principal, for embracing the opportunity for us to observe and write about what the Franconia teachers are doing in reading workshop. We toured the entire school, taking photos of the physical classroom environments the teachers and students had created for reading workshop. Catherine Gehman and Ursula Gamler, thank you for the time we spent in your two ELA classes at Gilbertsville Elementary in Boyertown Area School District experiencing students learning about book talks and having fun book talking their independent reads. We observed students trying out new protocols for book club sessions along with interactive read-alouds, minilesson and small group instruction, independent reading time, conferences, and end-of-workshop reflection. Principal Stephanie Petri, thanks for your hospitality and warm welcome. A big thank you to Kristin Haring, an ELA/reading teacher at Kutztown Area Middle School in Kutztown Area School District. Kristin's entire room is set up to grow readers!

We want to give a big shout-out to the educators and children's authors we interviewed—Janet Wong, Frank Murphy, Dr. Mwenyewe Dawan, Gail Ryan, and Dr. Aileen Hower. Thanks for giving up your time to share your thoughts with us and the readers of this book.

Thank you, Ralph Abbott, for your time spent taking videos and photos in the classrooms where we gathered wisdom, knowledge, and joy!

Thanks to our editor and dear friend, Bill Varner, for all his sage advice, encouragement, and willingness to read dozens of emails and meet with us on Zoom and conference calls. Your faith in us, Bill, kept us focused and writing during a difficult time for everyone in our country and all over the world. We also would like to thank the Stenhouse family. Emily Hawkins, your leadership at Stenhouse has made a difference in many lives! A big thank you to Shannon St. Peter and Nate Butler.

Your mentorship and hard work helped us pull this book together and introduce it to the world. Thanks to Susan Benner for help with final edits. Finally, a big thank you to Terry Thompson, our editor and friend, for shepherding this book through the final stages for publication. Your Zoom conferences, emails, and revision help were amazing! You managed to maintain a sense of humor throughout this process and kept this project moving forward. Thanks for believing in us and in our book!

From Brenda

A special thank you to the mentors in my life who have challenged me to always think about my teaching practice. You pushed me to embrace challenges head on, ask questions, and try new ideas. You have shaped my teaching—Ruby Pannoni, Andrea Fishman, Judith Jester Durante, and Gail Ryan.

Thanks to the many colleagues and friends at the West Chester Writing Project—Diane Dougherty, Richard Mitchell, Joan Shellenberger, Renee Martin, Gaetan Pappalardo, and Pauline Schmidt, as well as the many participants in summer writing institutes who re-energized my teaching life each summer. Thank you, Mary Buckelew, for your words of encouragement and friendship, and reminding me to always go forward with poise, dignity, and grace.

Thanks to the "girls" at Franconia Elementary—Marissa Moyer and Kathleen McLaughlin—for opening your classrooms to me, for trying many ideas with me, and for your patience. You are the best!

Thanks to my friend and teacher-cheerleader, Barry Lane. You have encouraged not only me but the many students and teachers at Franconia Elementary to be better people.

To my husband and best friend, Scott. Thanks for the long walks after sitting at a computer for hours, reminders of the impact teachers make on the lives of their students, and just being you—you are my rock.

To Bill Varner, thank you for giving me the opportunity to write beside Lynne. Your honest words, encouraging words, and wise words helped create this book.

To Terry Thompson, thank you so much for guiding me through the process of publishing a book. Your thoughts pushed my thinking and made the writing clear and engaging.

From Lynne

A big thank you to Dr. Mary Buckelew, retired director of the project and my dear friend. You always cheered us on! Thank you, Dr. Pauline Schmidt, Director of the West Chester Writing Project, for all your support.

To my co-authors of other Stenhouse projects, Rose Cappelli, Diane Dougherty, and Stacey Shubitz, I have learned so much from all of you. Each book project layered my experience writing professional books for teachers. Diane, I miss you every day! Thank you, my friends, for your patience and continued support. You are the best of the best!

To my family, thanks for just being you! Ralph, I could not have written this book without you by my side. You are my everything!

Bill, this is my eighth book with Stenhouse. You have been my editor for each and every one of them. I am so glad we have had the chance to get to know each other and grow a friendship that will last beyond the makings of a book. Thank you for always being honest, encouraging, and thoughtful. Your wisdom has helped me put all I know and what I have learned into words to help teachers I may never meet in person. You have helped me give back to the educational community at large, and I thank you from the bottom of my heart.

Terry, how can I thank you for your attention to detail, your patience, enthusiasm, contributions, and thoughtful, positive suggestions? You made this book a collaborative effort, and Brenda and I thank you for your perseverance and dedication to the completion of *Welcome to Reading Workshop*.

A Model to Help Students Become Readers

Children learn to read by reading . . . but not without instructional support. It's well known that in order to become thoughtful, strategic, proficient readers, children need to read.

– Debbie Miller,
No More Independent Reading Without Support

As you enter the classroom, no one seems to notice. Heads are down and hands are holding books of all shapes and sizes. As you circulate, you recognize familiar books: picture books like *Night Job* by Karen Hesse, *Tiara's Hat Parade* by Kelly Starling Lyons, and *My Papi Has a Motorcycle* by Isabel Quintero, mysteries such as the *A to Z Mysteries* books and the new *Legacy of the Inventor: A Timmi Tobbson Adventure* (a Solve-Them-Yourself Picture Mysteries book for boys and girls 8–12) by J. I. Wagner, and *Meet Yasmin!* by Saadia Faruqi from a popular series. Someone is reading a graphic novel—*White Bird* by R. J. Palacio; another student has a volume of poetry by Kate Coombs, and two boys are partner reading *Chomp! A Book About Sharks* by Melvin Berger. It's plain to see that students are encouraged to read texts that are part of their world, such as information-based texts, media selections, and graphic novels like *Tiny Titans #50* by Art Baltazar, along with the more traditional literary texts.

Students in this learning community have opportunities for purposeful talk with peers about the texts they are reading. Some are clustered in the back corner of the room on cushions and bean bag chairs, using six-inch voices to discuss their choices for book club and deciding how many pages they will read before they meet again. Another group of four students sit with their teacher on the carpet in the front of the room by the chart stand. They are part of a small group learning about strategies that proficient readers use to make sense of what they are reading. Today the teacher is talking about the power of visualization and making personal connections using a passage from *Outside, Inside* by LeUyen Pham.

A quick survey of the room reveals the focus on books—they are everywhere! A classroom library prominently displays bins labeled as animal stories, biographies and autobiographies, graphic novels and comic books, teacher's picks, students' picks, and picture books. Shelves are devoted to books in a series, mysteries, and poetry. One corner of the room has a "book nook" highlighting science fiction books such as *Spaced Out* (a Moon Base Alpha novel) by Stuart Gibbs and *Aliens for Breakfast* by Jonathan Etra and Stephanie Spinner. The ledge of the back whiteboard serves double duty, showcasing favorites and read-alouds, complete with student-written recommendations, displayed so that students can see the entire front cover.

At the tinkling of a bell, the students finish their last sentence or share their last thought, move back to their desks to put away materials, and make their way to the rug in the front of the room. The final sharing begins. Students talk about how they made use of independent reading time and something they learned about themselves as readers. Anna shares that she has discovered that she will reread a favorite book when it is hard to get started with something new. JaLia admits, "I had already started a new chapter book at home but had to stop reading it when I joined my book club. I was getting confused when I was trying to read two mysteries at the same time."

So much is happening inside this workshop. It seems to run itself. But clearly, there are established routines and rituals. Students are engaged

and comfortable. Everyone seems to know how to choose a book for independent reading time, and everyone seems to have an understanding of their own reading identity.

Why We Wrote This Book

In our combined experiences, we have witnessed how reading programs have been used as the curriculum instead of as a resource. We have watched teachers struggle to meet the needs of their readers through a one-size-fits-all approach. This book offers a model to help students become readers . . . the kind of readers we always talk about and dream of having in our classrooms. We want our students to choose reading as an activity—not all the time, or even most of the time—but we do want them to consider reading as a recreational activity outside of school to find out more about themselves, about others, and about the world. "Literature . . . helps readers develop the imaginative capacity to put themselves in the place of others—a capacity essential in a democracy, where we need to rise above narrow self-interest and envision the broader human consequences of political decisions" (Rosenblatt, cited in Kridel, 2000). In reading workshop, students have this opportunity to read widely, envision broadly, and develop the capacity to empathize with others.

To that end, our goal for writing this book is to help elementary school teachers create reading communities where students become engaged, joyful, and competent readers of both academic and recreational texts. This book is about the structures and routines that will enable every student to become literate through practices that build strong foundations. It is not a book about *how* to teach reading; rather, it offers ways to scaffold instruction that can include phonemic awareness, phonics, reading fluency, vocabulary development, and comprehension skills. In their groundbreaking work, Dr. Jan Burkins and Kari Yates (2021) encourage a balance of instructional methods, arguing that all students "need access to both the secrets of the alphabetic code and relevant experiences with text. They need both explicit information about how reading works and immersive experiences that show how to leverage reading and writing to change the world" (2). The reading workshop framework allows for both comprehension instruction and phonics instruction to co-exist. One does not trump the other. Both are important for growing readers. Our youngest readers benefit from strategic phonological instruction as well as learning strategies to make meaning from the text. Hand in hand, these two components work together to build competent readers. In a workshop, teachers use a variety of formats to meet the needs of the students—from whole group direct instruction to flexible small groups to one-on-one instruction in a conference. As with building a house that lasts over time, the reading classroom we offer to our students must be supported by sound practices and a framework that builds on timely skills and strategies from year to year. The scaffolds, structures, and routines highlighted in this book will help you create a reading classroom where students will find academic success, discovering the wonder, curiosity, and knowledge that can be found in the pages of a book.

What Our Book Has to Offer

We invite you to become a part of our reading workshop community as you read *Welcome to Reading Workshop* and consider the opportunities this approach has to offer you and the readers in your classroom. A reading workshop begins with the creation of a classroom community, one that honors all the readers in your classroom, a community where children know they are valued and respected by their teacher and peers. It is in this supportive, caring community that children grow their reading confidence and identity, learning to take risks as they become more confident readers. These readers know that you, their teacher, value reading and thinking and will offer them support as they move toward reading independence. They trust that you will lead them to book titles and genres that will match their interests and then talk to them about the reading experience. And they know that you can empathize with them when they struggle or flounder because you, teacher, are a reader, too, in this community. This idea of community is so critical we begin with a chapter offering suggestions

and ideas we have used to build classroom communities of readers and frequently call back to its foundational importance throughout the book.

This book describes key components of a reading workshop. It is our hope that by providing you with these detailed descriptions and explanations of classroom tools and routines we will better equip you to implement them into your classroom. To meet this goal, we thought about what this book could include to help teachers implement reading workshop with or without a mandated reading program in place and settled on three primary components:

- Concrete examples (peeks into classrooms with narratives, interviews, and video clips) of key practices—rituals and routines—in a reading workshop approach to K–6 reading blocks.

- Scaffolds and options to balance your existing curriculum requirements with a reading workshop approach that includes daily time for independent reading.

- Useful tips, strategies, and ideas regarding professional learning, classroom instruction and management, book selection, book sharing, and formative assessment.

Society is evolving at a rapid rate. We believe that today's students need to become proficient, critical readers in order to participate in a global society as competent citizens. We also believe that the reading instruction this requires cannot be taught through any one program. In a reading workshop approach, students develop a deeper understanding of what readers do, set goals and timelines for themselves, and monitor their own progress. Students make deliberate choices about their reading selections, book groups, and research projects. Small group instruction centers around strategies, genres, interests, and responses to what is read. These choices and practices build reading identities and lead to greater engagement and greater confidence. Our book presents practical tips and advice to help teachers create this type of thriving reading community.

Who Should Read This Book

Welcome to Reading Workshop is a book that will help teachers create a
community of readers in their classrooms, a place where children can
learn to read with confidence and become lifelong readers. If you are
a brand-new teacher, novice teacher, or veteran teacher, and want to
implement a reading workshop, you will find what you need in this book.
Descriptions of key components and structures, as well as video clips and
classroom snapshots, will provide a foundation for your work and help
you to implement a reading workshop with more confidence. Support
staff such as reading specialists, instructional coaches, interventionists,
paraprofessionals, and school leaders can benefit from the description of
the workshop components and structures as they support the teachers
they work with. Preservice teachers and teacher educators—both
undergraduate and graduate—can use this book to become acquainted
with a reading workshop model that will empower their students,
differentiate instruction, and help them rethink how they can best align
with their district's curriculum and state and national standards to grow
competent, joyful readers. Master teachers and administrators who work
with new teachers in their three-to-five-year induction programs will find
this book useful as they observe reading workshops and offer high-quality
feedback and support to their staff. Professional learning communities
and book clubs can use this book to grow confident, competent reading
teachers as they use the "Stop and Reflect" questions at the end of each
chapter and try out strategies and ideas in the "Something to Try" section.

We envision you reading and talking about this book with your
colleagues and creating your own reading/learning community that can
serve as an example of the power of reading workshop. We invite you to
connect with us, posting your questions and success stories across social
media and sharing your reading workshop journey using the hashtag
#WelcomeRW. Happy reading!

Chapter 1

A Welcoming Foundation for Readers

Reading workshop is a beautiful structure for kids to "come of age" as readers and develop a lifelong love of reading.

– Sonja Cherry-Paul, Colleen Cruz, and Mary Ehrenworth, *Making Reading Workshop Work*

How do people become lifelong readers? When you think about how you became a lifelong reader, what comes to mind? Leisurely visits to a library with a parent who loved to read? Sitting and reading a much-loved book on a summer afternoon? Exchanging books with a friend? Perhaps you think of early school reading in terms of reading groups, "sounding out" words, and may even recall the basal series used in your elementary classrooms. We started with *Dick and Jane* readers. But our love of reading often stems from time spent reading a favorite book. Do you remember the first book you fell in love with? A book you asked someone to read time and time again until you could read it yourself? Lynne's favorite was *The Little House* by Virginia Lee Burton. Brenda's was *Eddie the Dog Holder* by Carolyn Haywood. It was this desire to read our favorites that began our journey as readers. When we repeat something over and over again, we do it for the reward of the experience. Readers come back to reading because they gain something from it—they are entertained, they learn something new, or both! The teacher's goal is to foster each student's purpose and help them develop a reading habit that will last a lifetime.

Reading workshop is a stance . . . a lens . . . a belief. In workshop, we provide access to high-quality literature. We survey our students to meet their needs and interests with books. We confer, offer feedback, and listen closely to our students' conversations. We connect the work we do with authentic reading experiences. We guide students to become self-determining learners. This is the work of reading workshop.

In its most basic format, reading workshop is an instructional practice that allows all students to access texts and receive instruction that will enable them to learn strategies to become more proficient readers. But it can be so much more than that. We believe reading workshop is a multifaceted infrastructure; we believe the underlying hope is to grow readers who are empathetic and who build their moral compasses through their experiences with authentic, powerful texts.

Key Terms of Reading Workshop

- **Anchor charts.** Charts created by the teacher to support and synthesize the teaching and thinking of the class. Charts can illustrate, define, and/or provide steps to follow for skills, strategies, or procedures taught. Charts act as a scaffold for readers as they move toward independence and serve to make the thinking of the reading community visible and permanent.
- **Flexible Grouping.** A way to group students for short-term purposes that allows them to move in and out of groups as needed. The teacher can decide to group using the following structures: Random, Ability, Readiness, Learning style, Strategy/Skill, or Interest.
- **Formative Assessment.** Ongoing, authentic, and based on present needs, this kind of assessment is most useful to inform our instructional practices. Landrigan and Mulligan (2013) state that formative assessment helps both teachers and students to recognize what they know and what they don't know in a timely fashion. When that happens, students' needs can be addressed, and appropriate adjustments can be made to ensure success.
- **Frontloading Strategies.** Strategies a teacher can use to provide students with the background knowledge necessary for applying necessary skills, strategies, and behaviors to be successful in the day's learning.
- **Gradual Release Model.** A model of instruction that suggests that cognitive work should shift slowly and intentionally from teacher modeling to joint responsibility between teachers and students, to independent practice and application by the learner (Pearson and Gallagher, 1983).

- **Guided Practice.** In guided practice, the teacher strategically uses questions, prompts, and cues to facilitate student understanding. This can be part of the minilesson where students participate to demonstrate their understanding of a skill or strategy before they are released for independent reading. It can be even more effective with small groups that are convened based on instructional needs. Here, the teacher focuses on releasing responsibility to students while providing instructional scaffolds to ensure each student's success.

- **Guided Reading.** An instructional practice where teachers support a small group of students at their instructional level to read a text independently. This approach allows students to practice and refine their skills and strategies while they are in the presence of an expert that guides them as they read, talk, and think their way through a text. Students develop greater control over the reading process through the development of reading strategies, which assist decoding and construction of meaning.

- **Independent Reading Time.** A time when readers read self-selected books, with accuracy and meaning, using skills and strategies taught during the minilesson. During this time, the teacher is able to confer and meet with small groups.

- **Interactive Read-Aloud.** A read-aloud experience where children are invited to actively engage in listening and talking about the text throughout the reading. Interactive read-alouds can come from a wide variety of genres and should tap into the readers' interests. Teachers carefully select texts with a variety of rich vocabulary, illustrations (for primary students), and text features including photos and captions or illustrations with labels. These same texts can be used as part of the minilesson for reading workshop. Teachers guide conversations and thinking throughout the reading.

- **Mentor Texts.** Pieces of literature communities return to again and again to help young readers and writers learn how to do what they may not yet be able to do on their own. Students should be introduced to literature first as listeners. They need to hear and appreciate the story and characters or explore new information as well as the rhythms, words, and message. Only then can they return to a well-loved book and examine it through the eyes of a reader learning about skill and strategy use.

- **Minilesson.** A time for whole-class explicit instruction. It is usually 10 to 15 minutes in length at the beginning of the workshop. The lesson focuses on a skill, strategy, or procedure the teacher determines is needed by the community based on curriculum demands and assessment.

- **Reader's Notebook.** A notebook designed to contain a reader's responses to texts, teaching, and reading. It can also be used to practice a strategy or skill taught in a minilesson. The notebook allows readers to think and reflect on paper before sharing thoughts and reactions orally with the community or in small groups.

- **Reader's Conferences.** An opportunity for the teacher to meet with individual students and teach them based on their personalized goals or needs as readers.

- **Share Session.** A time scheduled for the community to come together and reflect on the work they have been doing as readers as they close the workshop for the day. During this time, students learn from each other and support each other as they grow as readers. Both goal setting and celebration are components of a share session.
- **Small Group Instruction.** An instructional practice where the teacher gathers three to five students to explicitly teach a predetermined skill or strategy. Children may be reading on different reading levels or in different texts, but they share a similar need or are working on a similar goal. This format may be used for both enrichment and intervention purposes.
- **Summative Assessment.** At the end of a unit of study, summative assessments are used to evaluate which students reached the learning targets or outcomes and which students did not. Since this type of assessment is considered post-instruction, the results are less positioned to help you customize instruction that helps each student grow as a reader in the moment; that is the job of formative assessment.

Figure 1.1 Readers at work! These students eagerly await independent reading–a time to dive into a good book, one they have selected. Choice is a key motivating factor.

Key Components

The workshop model makes time for students to read independently, time for the teacher and students to meet together, and time for reflection and goal setting on a daily basis. To make this possible, reading workshop has several key components that work flexibly together to meet the needs of the reading community. In "Making Reading Workshop Work," Cherry-Paul, Cruz, and Ehrenworth (2020) define three major components of the workshop approach: the minilesson, where teachers teach/model a reading strategy and give students time for guided practice (active engagement); the time to interact in book clubs, research clubs, and independent reading; and the time to share, reflect, and set goals. The reading workshop model and its key components create frameworks for individualized, small group, and whole group instruction where everyone is a reader. The components fit together seamlessly, providing children with the opportunity to grow their reading identity. The diagram in **Figure 1.2** highlights the grounding structure of the workshop, and we consider some critical components that support instruction within it below.

Figure 1.2 A look at reading workshop: how it all fits together.

Minilessons (10–15 minutes)
Usually first to state the purpose, but can come later. Follows the Gradual Release of Responsibility Model including an opportunity for guided practice.

Read-Alouds
At various times throughout the day to introduce concepts, strategies, new genres, build vocabulary, and model what a fluent reader looks like. Interactive read alouds can be part of the minilesson.

Reflection & Sharing
(5–8 minutes)
Options for Reflection:
• Book talks
• Book reviews
• Readers' notebooks and logs

Status of the Class
(2–3 minutes)
Status of the class can occur after the minilesson or at the end of workshop.
Used as a formative assessment to track the reading processes of students.

Independent Reading (Small Groups, Conferring) (30–40 minutes)
Students read, respond to texts with partnerships in clubs as written and oral response.
Teachers observe reading behaviors by clipboard cruising and conferring with 3–8 students before starting small group work.
Options for Small Groups:
• Book Clubs   • Research   • Enrichment   • Strategy Review
• Special Interests • Intervention   • Genre Study   • Reader's Theater

MINILESSONS

Reading workshop includes explicit teaching based on students' needs in phonemic awareness/phonics skills, comprehension, fluency, and/or vocabulary. This teaching occurs initially in minilessons and is then revisited in small or whole group settings and individual conferences. Minilessons center on high-quality mentor texts that represent different genres, organizational structures, and the faces of your reading community.

INDIVIDUAL CONFERENCES

A major focus of reading workshop is an emphasis on process over product. Conferring informs the practices the teacher will invite students to try. Listening to students talk about their reading enables you to help them choose books and can help create a love of reading while giving you opportunities to offer personalized instruction and feedback. Conferring positions the reader as the expert on their reading work; the most important person in the room at that moment in time.

TIME TO REFLECT AND TALK

Children have regular and ongoing time to talk with their peers about their books and their ideas while also learning how to work in partnerships, take turns reading and talking, and adjust the volume of their voice to an appropriate level. They learn about each other's reading interests and often make recommendations in the form of book reviews and book talks. At the end of workshop, students gather to reflect on their independent reading and strategy use and to make connections with other readers.

ROUTINES AND RITUALS

Structures are in place to allow children to celebrate each other's progress and successes and give you a variety of opportunities to provide critical feedback. Small groups meet periodically and are flexible in nature, allowing for movement based on interests, genres, and skill or strategy work. Anchor charts support students' conversations and thinking.

These charts are often generated on the run, as students study vocabulary, phonics, and genres and investigate comprehension strategies. Throughout all of this, sharing and reflection naturally occur. That is the beauty of a workshop approach: routines and rituals seamlessly and effectively overlap and support the overall structure of the model.

READING VOLUME

Stephen Krashen (2004), in his book *The Power of Reading*, finds that the single greatest factor in reading achievement, even above socio-economics, is reading volume—how much reading people do. In a workshop, readers read A LOT! Independent reading is a key component, and workshop builds in time for students to do the work of independent readers daily. There is an expectation that children will read books that are a good fit for them, reading with 95% accuracy, with fluency and comprehension intact. Allington, McCuiston, and Billen (2015) state, "evidence accumulated suggests that texts that can be read with 95% or greater accuracy are directly, and in some studies causally, related to improved reading achievement" (499). Time spent in a reading workshop allows students to acquire vocabulary, fluency, and strategies needed to support their reading work as they encounter texts of greater complexity. It is the expectation that all members of the community *work* to meet goals, set new goals, and take risks as readers. Learning about new series, genres, and formats, such as graphic novels, helps spark interest and deepens engagement.

TEACHER TIP: Encouraging reading outside of school is another way to build reading volume and helps students to value reading as a real-world activity, not just something they do in school. The home–school connection is vital. Help parents understand the school expectations for outside reading, the nature of reading workshop, and strategies that they can use at home when they read to and with their child. Parent education and parent engagement are vital.

Figure 1.3 Jamie chooses books to read based on his interest and ability. He has access to a wide variety of texts and finds the books that meet his needs.

INTEREST AND CHOICE

In reading workshop children have access to high-quality, high-interest books that will comfort them, challenge them, entertain them, and help them learn about the world in which they live. As teachers, we help students make choices about what to read and strategies to work on and incorporate as they read. By providing readers with quick, easy access to a book collection filled with different genres, authors, writing styles, perspectives, and experiences, we ensure that readers' choices and identities are honored. In this way, teachers help students build their sense of agency as readers.

READING PROCESSES

Reading is a skill that is constantly evolving, and the workshop approach makes room for this evolution. Reading involves an interactive, problem-solving collaboration between the reader, the text, and the reader's purpose for reading. As a complex process, we read with our background of knowledge and experiences related to a particular text. A text evokes knowledge and memories. Depending on our comfort level with the text, we may be able to dive in and read the text from start to finish with little or no rereading. But if we are dipping into unfamiliar topics, genres, and organizational formats, our reading is likely to be more deliberate; we slow down and have many false starts while we try to relate the material to our existing background knowledge and understandings. We revise our thinking and understanding as we read, leaving the text with a different perspective than when we first entered it. Our thinking has been transformed, changed by the encounter with the text. Effective readers understand the processes of reading and consciously control them. This awareness is called metacognition or knowing about what you know—understanding your own thought processes.

Reading, like writing, is not a linear process. We problem-solve, not just from the words on the page but from the memories and content knowledge we associate with the words and sentences on a given page. We may backtrack—reread previous paragraphs or pages—and even have internal conversations with ourselves. We continue to monitor our comprehension, and in the end, we come to realize that our reading process is far from solitary and finite. It is an interaction of many voices—the author's voice and the reader's voice—and all the voices that are mixed into the equation as readers come together to talk about the text as a community of readers.

BECOMING LIFELONG READERS

Perhaps most important of all, children must first see themselves as readers, talk about themselves as readers, and set authentic and realistic goals for themselves as readers. You, the teacher, share your own reading life with your students and use engaging methods that motivate them to read, such as book talks, book trailers, book reviews, and read-alouds, creating an excitement for books and reading. In this way, you are a model of what it means to be a lifelong reader. A reading workshop offers an environment full of opportunities for students to experience the joy of what it means to live a readerly life. In all of this, the workshop model invites the learning community into a shared world of reading, allowing teachers and students to make important decisions for future instruction, grow together, and celebrate literacy as lifelong readers.

A Familiar Structure with a Flexible Approach

A workshop philosophy makes room for you to blend elements from many resources, philosophies, and texts. In addition to its ability to efficiently address literacy standards and meet the varied needs of the learners in your reading community, the workshop approach encourages flexibility based on the direct needs of both. The familiar structure and key components of reading workshop fit seamlessly into any language arts block. As you read this book, consider the strategies and tips we offer and think about how you might adjust routines and structures as needed to meet the needs of the diverse population that sits before you.

For instance, you can easily incorporate your district's chosen anthology into your workshop text collection. Anthologies often group selections around text types, so they can be great resources to introduce themes, genres, authors, and even some nonfiction texts within the workshop setting. Your anthology selection can also be used to extend your book clubs, literature circles, and even research projects. Supplementing with books from the library to support students' understanding of a genre through immersion during independent reading time is a great way to integrate your anthology in reading workshop.

As we mentioned previously, explicit phonics instruction, in a systematic way, can easily occur within the workshop during a minilesson, reinforced through flexible small group instruction and in individual conferences, and then transferred to partner and independent reading experiences. Readers need to be taught to use multiple sources of information, including letters and letter sounds, and a responsive reading workshop makes room for this. In the primary grades, small decodable texts can be used to build confidence and help students move beyond them to more complex texts that align with their personal interests while providing authentic reading experiences. The differentiated instruction inherent in the reading workshop approach creates a space where students who need explicit phonics instruction will get it, even in upper elementary grades.

The adjustments you could make within the familiar workshop structure are boundless. You can rearrange the instructional order (e.g., starting with independent reading and saving your minilesson for a mid-workshop teaching point), get creative with amount of time you spend on the segments (e.g., scheduling an extended time for end-of-workshop sharing), or rethink the ways you spread your workshop across your instructional week (e.g., holding a longer workshop on Tuesday because of Monday's assembly). When you build your workshop around the specific needs of the reading community in front of you, you can't go wrong!

Final Thoughts

In the chapters that follow, we will bring you directly in touch with classroom examples, teacher tips, and instructional options. As you read, notice interactions between teachers and students, and students with their peers. Start to ask questions. *Why is this important? Does this look like my classroom or does this look very different? How can this help me grow as a teacher? How could I make time and space for this in my classroom?*

Reading workshop provides an ongoing opportunity to build and sustain a community of learners, connect with others, and move forward together in knowledge and skill set. It develops competence in all readers in an environment that sustains and supports them through best practice, including authentic reading experiences, ongoing feedback, and time to read!

Stop and Reflect

1. Who stood by you as you became a reader? How did their presence in your reading life affect you as a reader?
2. Who are your reading mentors today? What communities of readers guide your thinking and/or help you challenge yourself as a reader? How do your mentors help you value the time you invest in reading? How do they help you celebrate the joy of reading?

Something to Try

Begin keeping track of your own reading. Create your own system or use an app or website such as Goodreads. This practice will help you identify the genres you read, your attention to interests, the time you've spent reading, and attention to nonfiction and fiction. With this knowledge, you can set goals for yourself. Are you only reading fiction? Maybe it's time to search for a good nonfiction read.

Chapter 2

Building a Community of Readers

A community of readers is a group of people who share the common goal of reading and discussing literature and becoming literate human beings. The community is built on mutual respect and a willingness on the part of each participant to listen to and consider the merits of each member's ideas and interpretations.

– Frank Serafini,
Around the Reading Workshop in 180 Days

On a warm August evening, Brenda sits with her computer and a handful of envelopes. She eagerly opens the first envelope and begins to read. "Thank you for asking about our daughter Claire . . ." the letter begins. Each year Brenda sends a small survey along with her welcome-back-to-school letter to the parents, caregivers, or guardians of her incoming students. She asks them to introduce their precious children to her by describing them and answering some simple questions. What are your child's interests? Likes and dislikes? Strengths and needs? What are your hopes and dreams for your child this year? And *what does your child like to read?* Brenda reads each letter and questionnaire, taking notes, in preparation for meeting each student. These little tidbits of information will help Brenda find books for her students on day one. Reading each letter begins the process of creating a classroom community of readers.

Creating a lifelong reader begins with our classroom community: a place where readers can meet, discuss, debate, and borrow each other's ideas; a place where readers know their thoughts are valued and their voices will be heard; a place where teachers demonstrate that they live a readerly life—sharing their passion for reading with their students. Of course, helping students become lifelong readers requires in-class time to read independently. But they'll need more than time. How do we build a safe place for all readers? It starts with an empty classroom that is full of promise.

Creating a Safe Place for All Readers

Developing a sense of safety is fundamental to a community of readers. In order to help students become more engaged, strategic readers, we need to hear from them about what is going on in their minds as they are reading. Our readers should feel comfortable about relating their excitement, confusion, disagreement, and even their disengagement with texts. They should understand that different readers bring different resources and perspectives that help the community interpret and deepen their understanding of complex texts.

In a safe place, readers understand that their ideas, thoughts, and questions have a place in classroom conversations. They know that their thinking is valued and makes a difference. In this community, risk-taking can become commonplace, encouraged, and fostered. Regie Routman (2018, 52) encourages us to see the classroom through our students' eyes. In *Literacy Essentials: Engagement, Excellence, and Equity for All Learners*, Routman states, "If we truly want students to excel, we need to be sure the setting, tone, and classroom culture encourage and enhance risk taking, deep conversations, and meaningful learning." Who are the readers who enter our classrooms on the first day of school, and how do we create a safe community where they can thrive?

Getting to Know Our Students

Our readers come to school with individual tastes and desires. They see themselves as readers of comic books, chapter books, pictures books, and magazines. However, there are many students who do not read and do not care to join the "literacy club" (Smith 1988, 12). Our job is to find out as much as we can about these readers and welcome them to our reading community. We can begin with an easy-to-use interest survey or simply have a whole group discussion about the kinds of books we enjoy reading (see Appendices A: Book Recommendations to Help Build and Celebrate a Reading Community; B: Four Square Interest Survey, 3–6; and C: Reading Interest Survey, Grades K–2). Sharing books on topics that appeal to the age level and the cultural identities of our students is one way of building interest. We could ask students to join us in creating a bulletin board to advertise our favorites—books we've read and returned to more than once. We might also ask students to share an autobiographical sketch of their reading identity (see **Figure 2.1**). The idea here is to get kids talking about books in positive ways while sharing their reading identities and interests.

Figure 2.1 Fourth graders create autobiographical sketches as they respond to questions that help them think about their reading identity.

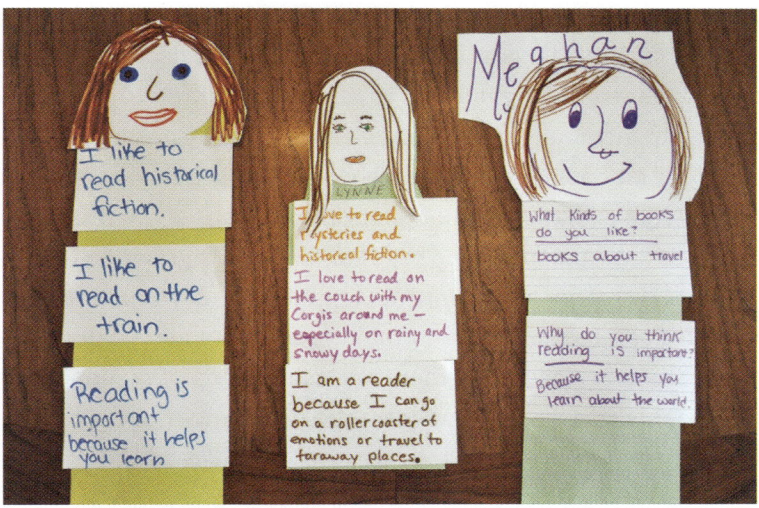

What Is Reading Workshop?

Reading workshop, to me, is (more than anything else) an opportunity. An opportunity to create connections and relationships, readers-to-readers and readers-to-books. And maybe even readers-to-possibilities. Reading workshop informs me about my young readers in ways that no other device in school can (except for a writers' workshop!). Albert Einstein once said, "In the middle of difficulty lies opportunity"; reading workshop can be difficult to start and manage and sustain, but the opportunities that lie within are priceless.

Frank Murphy,
Grade 6 ELA teacher and children's author, Council Rock School District

We can begin to establish a community of readers with a review of students' past reading habits, in school and out of school. We might place students into small groups to give mini–book talks about what they read last year or over the summer during the first few weeks of school. Teachers may want to sit in on one or several groups to informally evaluate students, listening to conversations and writing down important observations. These observations can lead to individual reading conferences where teachers learn more about students' reading habits, what they take away from a book, and how they handle reading challenges on their own. These conversations can help us set goals for the first few weeks of school. The goal here is to learn a great deal about our new students as readers right away. By allowing children to talk about the books they've already read and value, we eliminate the pressure to "correctly" choose a first book during reading workshop. When we spend time giving our students a chance to chat about their favorites, we immediately create a positive tone, partnerships begin to form (kids gravitate to other kids who read the same books, author, or genre), and we've already conducted formative assessment without making students feel anxious.

In any one classroom, there are many kinds of readers. We want all our students to accept and respect the preferences of their peers. Reading workshop is the safe place that we celebrate *all* readers for the choices

they make and the reading they do, not just the readers who have read the greatest number of pages or the highest number of books. It means the community celebrates with Seth and Alia when they finish their first chapter book as third graders or when Drew, a fifth grader, shares that he has just finished reading an entire book for the first time by Halloween.

Building a Community through Conversation: Learning to Listen and Respond

In our reading workshop, we usually designate a place where readers can gather as a community to have readerly conversations and learn from each other. This closeness is one way to help students bond and it provides an opportunity to learn how to talk to each other. It is through these conversations that a community begins to form as children talk with many peers and as a class, letting others' thinking in and growing their reading identities (**Figure 2.2**).

Figure 2.2 Third graders share their thinking about their independent reading choices.

In *Reading Essentials* (2003), Routman encourages us to create structures that maximize participation and learning. These include small group discussions about books in literature circles and book clubs, student-led literature discussions, partner reading, and shared reading opportunities. Learning how to maximize our time for conversations instead of teacher-led Q&As will help students build confidence and develop their unique voices. Brenda begins by modeling how to turn and talk, intentionally helping children learn to face each other, make eye contact, and listen to each other's ideas and opinions, then how to respond to each other. All voices must be heard.

We try to make initial conversations non-threatening and light—*Where did you read last night? What is surprising to you in the read-aloud? Which character in our read-aloud would you like to have lunch with?* (See **Appendix A: Book Recommendation Choices to Help Build and Celebrate a Reading Community.**)

As the children become more comfortable with each other, we can support their conversations with more personal connections to what is being read as well as personal insights. We ask children to share their conversations, sometimes asking them to share their partner's thinking rather than their own—which feels safer for many kids (especially in the beginning of the year) and also requires them to be active listeners. During these conversations (as well as instructional time and in individual conferences), it is helpful if the teacher refers to the class as readers. "Readers, today as we gather on the rug to begin reading workshop, I would like you to think about the reasons you choose a book to read on your own." By calling our students "readers" as often as possible, we highlight this part of their identity and—if they're not quite there yet—invite them to begin to see themselves as readers. Bringing our class together as a community to talk about books and reading sends the message that we are all learning to read together.

READERLY CONVERSATIONS ACROSS THE YEAR

To continually grow your readers, we suggest prioritizing time during your busy workshop routine to have readerly conversations all year. This involves a whole class discussion with opportunities for you to record the thinking of the community on an anchor chart. In **Figure 2.3**, we include some important conversation starters to help move these community discussions forward. Pick and choose the ones that seem appropriate to your grade level and students. These conversations can be repeated at different times throughout the year when you feel a need to bring the community together around a topic, to reinvigorate your workshop, and to highlight the community's thinking about reading on anchor charts to make it visible and permanent.

In Brenda's classroom the children regularly revisited the question *Why is reading important?* The conversations grew more sophisticated as the year progressed and often helped students set new goals. These conversations can be used as formative assessment—to help deepen your understanding of your students as readers and to give them time to reflect on important ideas, concerns, and strengths as developing readers. These conversations could occur once or twice a month, or as needed. When leading readerly conversations, try to talk less and listen more. Let the students lead so their responses are genuine and not tempered by your thinking. It's our students' voices we want to hear in these discussions.

Figure 2.3

Ten Readerly Conversation Starters

1. What do readers do? What habits help someone become a lifelong reader?
2. What are your reasons for reading?
3. How do you share books you've read with others?
4. How do you choose a reading goal? What are your personal goals for reading? What goal are you working on right now?
5. How are nonfiction books different from fiction books? How do you change your reading process to read nonfiction?
6. Who are your models for reading? How does that help you?
7. Where do you focus your attention when you read? On the characters? The action? The conflict? The connections with your own life? What is going on in the world?
8. How is your reading life at home the same as or different from your reading life at school? What could make it easier to read at home? Do you have a spot at home to read?
9. Why is reading important? Does everyone need to be a reader? Why do you think so?
10. How does reading help you deepen your understanding of your family, your community, and the world?

TEACHER TIP: When working with primary students, choose your questions in ways that inherently generate more conversation. Try for responses that will allow children to hear comments they may have thought but didn't know how to express.

LEARNING TO LISTEN

Listening is the gateway to understanding in classrooms, work relationships, and personal relationships. It is one of the critical communications skills along with reading, writing, and speaking. We often address listening by tucking it in with other instructional practices, but learning to listen and respond must be modeled and taught to students. In today's world, dominated by social media and texting, there is less opportunity to engage in conversation to hone our listening and speaking skills. Teaching children to notice how words can show respect, kindness, and empathy for others becomes important minilessons in the beginning of the year. Students are also more likely to listen to someone they know on a personal level than to someone who they do not. Take the time to really get to know your students, their hobbies, who their friends are, and so on by using interest surveys and interviews, and by creating a mailbox where students can leave notes for you. Too often, students have only practiced Q&As in school. When we allow students to form partnerships, participate in book clubs and literature discussions, and engage in end-of-workshop reflections, we are building better listeners. Teaching our students how to listen involves practicing strategies such as asking for clarification, making eye contact, and actually being present in the conversation—using body language to give the speaker your full attention. In a discussion, ask partners to summarize what they are hearing and ask a question like, "Is this what you wanted to say?" or "Did I leave out anything important?" Sometimes, a reader-responder may simply ask, "Could you explain more about _____" or "I am not sure I understand _____. Can you tell me more?" As teachers we can model this behavior when we chat with our students about nonacademic topics as well as when we confer with them more formally.

ACTIVE LISTENING

Instead of thinking of listening as a passive experience, we need to view it as an essential part of what we actively do to make meaning and strengthen our learning community. In his book *Opening Minds: Using Language to Change Lives* (2012), Peter Johnston says, "Listening is the foundation of a conversation, and it requires that we are open to the possibility of changing our thinking" (102). He reminds us that by listening we become responsive to the speaker and their ideas. As children learn to listen, they develop new ideas and ways of thinking that may differ from their own.

To demonstrate how conversations connect community, Lynne asked a group of fourth grade students to pull up their chairs and join her in a small circle. The rest of the class stood behind them in a larger circle. The students were ready to talk about *The Other Side* by Jacqueline Woodson (2001), a book Lynne had previously shared as a read-aloud. Lynne began by talking about the title of the book and why she thought the author had chosen it. Lynne had a big ball of soft, blue yarn. When Marie spoke, Lynne held onto the end of a piece of yarn and passed the ball of yarn to Marie, letting a single strand stretch between her and her student. As the students listened to each other and layered their responses, they passed the ball of yarn back and forth, creating an interesting pattern of threads that connected Lynne and the students. This visual exercise had a powerful effect on the students. They could see how a conversation involves keen listening to make connections and build upon the ideas that are presented.

One way to promote active listening is to have students share their partner's thinking rather than their own after a turn-and-talk. You could assign who talks first by asking the person who sits on your right to speak first or the person whose birthday is coming soon or who has the shortest hair. Students may need scaffolds to help them structure their conversations. Often, it is helpful to set some guidelines:

- Ask listeners to avoid thinking about their response while the other person talks. And simply listen; that is all.

- To avoid interrupting, show listeners how to jot down a key word or two on a sticky note as a memory jogger for something they would like to comment about.

- When the student stops talking, the other takes a breath before speaking and begins by paraphrasing something their partner just said: "You believe that . . ."; "You aren't sure if. . . ."

- After paraphrasing their partner, they can then follow that with an "I" statement: "I see what you mean. . . "; "I'm not sure I agree . . . because. . . ." Finally, the partner can add their thinking to the discussion.

Good listeners are both rare and valued. It's important to share this with students, and to also share the fact that people who really listen—make eye contact, show interest, and restrain from interrupting others in a conversation—are easy to like and respect.

THE ART OF DISCUSSION

Just as we teach our students to listen, they need to be taught the art of discussion. Teaching children what a discussion is and its value helps them understand the importance of considering points of view and ideas that may be different from what they know or have learned in the past. Turner and Paris (1995) explain that open-ended tasks that include the kinds of questions we ask students to respond to help them to choose and organize information as well as to assess outcomes and set goals, all essential to rich discussions. Anchor charts such as the ones presented in **Figure 2.4** can detail what is important to remember as a speaker and a listener.

Figure 2.4

Discussion Guidelines Chart

A. Stick to the topic.
B. Pay attention to the person talking.
C. Ask questions about ideas given.
D. Give everyone a chance to participate.
E. Try not to interrupt others.

Our Discussion Goals

1. All members of the group participate in the discussion.
2. Everyone demonstrates active listening skills.
3. Everyone expresses ideas freely without fear of getting teased.
4. All responses show that you are thinking!

What a Discussion Is and Is Not

Discussion Is	Discussion Is Not
• Supporting ideas with text • Discussing feelings • Sharing and listening to opinions • Making predictions • Noticing author's craft • Raising important/interesting questions • Learning from each other • Making connections with text and with other community members • Understanding there are many ways to approach a problem and solve it	• Conversation that wanders or strays from the topic • Reporting or simply retelling • Just repeating facts, as if you were taking a test • Dominated by one or two people in the group • Debating • Putting forth "only one right way to do something"

Classroom conversations allow community members to grow in new ways because they develop a knowledge base grown from ideas shared by all the children, helping them to imagine new ways to solve problems, think about and share literature, and respond with curiosity and empathy.

Figure 2.5 An example of an anchor chart created by Brenda's third graders after they discussed what conversations look like, sound like, and feel like.

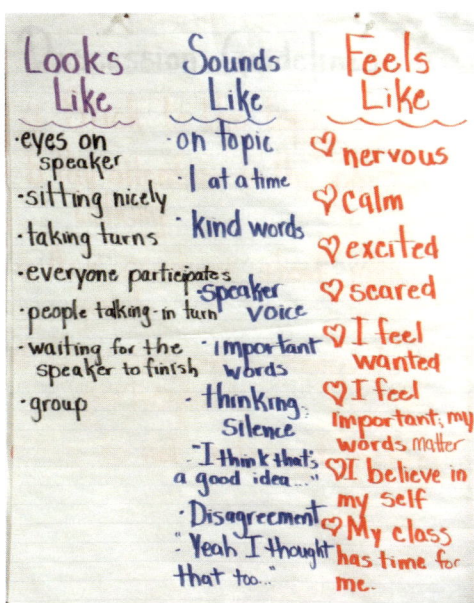

Who I Am as a Reader: Building a Reader Identity

Not all children come to school believing they are readers or that they will be accepted into a community of readers. But, as Val Kimmel shares in her contribution to *Game Changer! Book Access for All Kids* (Donalyn Miller and Colby Sharp 2018), "We must create literary communities that 'tell' kids who they are so they can develop habits and dispositions that establish their identity as a reader. An identity that will serve them now and well into adulthood" (126). Being part of the academic club of readers and writers is not always easy, but there are simple things teachers can do to raise awareness and promote students as readers.

Figure 2.6 A fifth grade student demonstrates she is a reader through pictures and words by creating a map of her reading life.

If you could describe yourself as a reader, how would you begin? What would you say? What would feel most important to highlight? To help kids celebrate their reading identities, find ways for them to talk about their readerly life with each other, to write about it, and to reflect on possible goals and challenges as they move forward. One way to document this information is to have students create a map of their reading life where they share graphics and words to illustrate who they are as readers. Creating and sharing our own map as adults serves as a model and shows that we are also readers in our community. Other options could include trifolds, timelines, autobiographical sketches, and interest surveys.

On the first day of school, students could complete trifolds with pictures, titles, and even words to describe books they read last year, books they are currently reading, and books they have in waiting. These trifolds can be displayed at eye level in the classroom. Encourage students to initial or sign their names in squares that name books they would like to talk about with the classmate who created that trifold. Remember, let students know they could include comic books, magazines, cookbooks, or even video game instructions to represent reading items on their trifolds.

Creating timelines allows readers to see their histories as readers. Upper elementary readers can use these to reflect on their continual growth as readers and set goals for the coming year. Teachers can model this with their own timelines. As students look at their timelines, help them think about genres they are reading a lot and some they are not reading. Are they reading books that are all fiction and avoiding nonfiction? Where do they spend most of their time? Timelines can also be used for reflection during reading experiences. Adding the title and a reflection bubble to their reading responses gives readers a chance to reflect on things they learned, strategies they relied on, or things they learned about themselves as readers while reading the books.

Autobiographical sketches of students' reading lives help them think about their reading identities (see **Figure 2.7**). Here, students can reflect on their lifelong reading journeys and then write about their successes and failures, their joys, and their fears by creating poetry, six-word memoirs, friendly letters, cartoon drawings, or even newspaper articles—whatever way they feel most comfortable sharing their reading pasts.

Figure 2.7 A map of Kyla's reading life.

> **TEACHER TIP:** Primary students can reflect on their reading identities by sharing favorite stories they have read with parents, older siblings, grandparents, or even babysitters. Many of them have favorites that they have read repeatedly. Ask parents to provide titles of much-loved books and stories so your youngest readers can see themselves as readers.

Finding books readers identify with strongly helps them understand the power of a book and the importance of making a personal connection that could last a lifetime. One way to help students see the powerful books their community members are reading is by taking photographs of students with their books, and then inviting them to discuss the meaning of those books for them. After readers share their photos aloud with their peers, they can post them with their thoughts inside speech bubbles. These declarations give us glimpses into the reading identities of the readers in our classrooms and help us make thoughtful choices about books to recommend, lessons to teach, and ways to grow our community.

Interest surveys (see **Appendices B** and **C**) can also reveal many things about the readers in your classroom. What are their favorite genres? Authors? How much time do they spend reading when they are not in school? As we learn more about our individual readers, we can start to reimagine our classroom libraries, choices for read-alouds, and daily instruction in ways that value all the readers in our classes.

Who We Are as a Community of Readers

Once we understand more about our readers and their individual tastes and habits, we can begin to create a collective identity as a community of readers, and one of the strongest foundations for this is the whole class read-aloud. Gathering around one book, readers share a collective experience along with thoughts, opinions, insights, questions, and emotions while growing together as a community of readers (see **Chapter 3**). In addition to being a treasured time that teachers and students look forward to each day, reading aloud gives children lots of opportunities to practice listening—a crucial skill for kindergarten and beyond. It exposes children to rare words and ideas not often found in everyday conversations (Varlas 2018). An interactive read-aloud gives students a chance to notice all the ways different readers think aloud and respond to texts as they work to understand their purpose and message. It gives students the opportunity to notice the different kinds of background knowledge and experience that their classmates and their teacher bring to texts. Most of all, it creates the foundation for shared knowledge about books and authors that every member of the reading community identifies with.

Figure 2.8 The "Read-Aloud Bookshelf" posted outside Brenda's classroom advertises what she is currently reading to her students during read-aloud time.

Book talks are another way to provide opportunities to build a community of readers. The activity of children sharing favorite titles with their peers creates a buzz about books that becomes contagious. In sharing books, children share their reading identities. (see **Chapter 6** for a more in-depth discussion on book talks.) Together, communities build a sense of collaborative and respectful inquiry by sharing their likes and dislikes, their reading processes, and their habits.

For all of us, sharing our thinking within a supportive, shared community can help us to pay closer attention to things that may go unnoticed. We start to clearly understand what effective readers do as they read. We notice and appropriate the successful strategies and problem-solving skills of our peers as we grow as a community of readers.

Final Thoughts

With teaching lessons, preparing for standardized tests, and helping to ensure that students attain certain benchmarks, equally important things like building a strong classroom community can take a back seat. Still, a strong classroom community is integral to students' success in school.

In reading workshop, students learn how to have real conversations and establish doable guidelines for a respectful exchange of ideas. Starting the year with conversations about past reading experiences, conferring with students as they explore their attitudes about reading, and getting to know readers through interest surveys and conferences are important foundations for reading instruction that will establish your reading communities with a love of books and reading. Although these practices require some time, in the end they will save you time! Growing independent readers who are confident and willing to take risks to try new genres, authors, and reading strategies stems from a joyful classroom culture that encourages collaboration, a sense of ownership and identity, and a feeling of belonging to a community of readers.

Stop and Reflect

1. How do you help your students create a reading identity? What kinds of activities could you use to help students think about who they are as readers and how they are growing and changing as readers?

2. How would you describe your current classroom community of readers? Engaged? Thriving? Excited? Emerging? Why? How would you sustain or change it?

Something to Try

Create a map, timeline, or autobiographical sketch of your own reading life. What did you learn about yourself as a reader? How would sharing your reading journey with your students support their own growth as readers?

Chapter 3

The Power of Read-Alouds and Mentor Texts to Inspire Community and Support the Reading Workshop

Too often children (and some adults) consider the read-aloud as a time to doze, dream, fiddle, and snack. I see the read-aloud as the heart of our reading instruction time, and I want kids' full attention to be on what we do together.

– Lucy Calkins,
The Art of Teaching Reading

Sitting on the carpet, the class is still . . . quiet. Not a whisper. Eyes focus on the teacher. Time is at a standstill (or so it seems). The page turns, Brenda stops reading, and moves to close the book.

"No, not now," a voice calls. "There are only a few pages left. We have to find out what happens to Pax. Please keep reading, Mrs. Krupp."

Brenda pauses to let this sink in. She has a choice to make: finish the book or keep her schedule and begin math.

"Please!" a new voice pleads.

She looks over the remaining pages. "Well, I don't know if I can keep reading," she explains. The children look at her, questioning her words. "We are at the end and there are only two ways this book can end." Another pause to let these words sink in. Heads nod, acknowledging they understand.

Logan, sitting at her feet, looks at her intently. The class has been reading *Pax* (2019) by Sara Pennypacker. Children, beginning to understand and consider how the ending could go, whisper to each other. Then Brenda says, "You know I am definitely going to cry either way. . . ." Suddenly a box of tissues appears at her feet.

"Okay, Mrs. Krupp, now you're ready. Please read us the ending," Logan says, handing her an individual tissue and patting her on the back.

Why Do We Read Aloud?

Reading aloud supports many purposes (see **Figure 3.1**), but perhaps the single most important reason to read aloud to your students is to foster engagement and a passion for reading. In Chapter 2 we talked about the importance of read-alouds as a way to build and sustain a community of readers. The read-alouds we return to many times in reading and writing workshops help students develop a sense of belonging. According to Peter Johnston (Reading Recovery Conference of North America, 2013), "We have to create classrooms where the learning community helps build the minds within it. Teaching children to think together builds reasoning, comprehension, expressive language, and creative thinking". We believe read-alouds do this and more.

Figure 3.1

A Rationale for Reading Aloud

- Demonstrates purposes for reading and that print is meaningful
- Introduces new authors, titles, genres, organizational structures, and topics to foster a love and commitment to reading
- Demonstrates the power of story—that we can be moved to change or moved to action
- Creates a classroom community around books while modeling what a fluent reader looks like and sounds like
- Builds rapport between teacher and students as they grow a lifelong commitment to reading
- Gives teachers a chance to "think aloud" in order to make the process of comprehension visible

- Gives teachers a chance to practice a strategy with students, providing insights into how reading works
- Stimulates language development and imagination through an appreciation of imagery and words
- Helps to widen students' views of themselves, of others, and of the world through a shared text experience
- Helps readers see things they may have missed had they not had a shared experience

When Do We Read Aloud?

Read-alouds are a cherished and necessary part of daily classroom time. Lester Laminack (2019) reminds us that the shared read-aloud is a time in the day when the community comes together around a common text. "When a teacher reads aloud, it is a bonding between the teacher, the children, the books and the act of reading." Children eagerly await read-aloud time, as do their teachers. Reading aloud can happen at any time during the school day, can occur more than once across the day, and can be anything from a poem to a chant to sustained time with a beloved chapter book. Reading aloud can occur as a way to open the day with the community gathered close to you, before or after lunch or recess, when students are lining up to move to art, gym, library class, and other specials, or as the last activity before the students go home as a positive community close to the day for all.

Dr. Steven Layne (2015, 36), literacy consultant, motivational keynote speaker, and author, advises us to protect our daily read-aloud time. He believes that when we cancel read-aloud because of special assemblies, early dismissals, or simply because we feel we have fallen behind, we are basically telling students that the read-aloud has less value than other instructional practices. We not only let our students down, we become somewhat unreliable in their eyes; and sadly, read-aloud time becomes less important to them as well. Through our commitment to read-alouds, we demonstrate that reading a book from cover to cover is well worth the effort!

Figure 3.2 Sharing books together on National Read-Aloud Day, held every February, introduces new books to students and builds community.

Texts shared during read-alouds can also do double duty as mentors that will be revisited later during reading workshop for instructional purposes. Sharing a mentor text during your read-aloud time outside of workshop can save valuable time for whole-group and small-group instruction, independent reading, and reflection in workshop space. Since readers will already be familiar with the text, you can return to it the next day or week to teach a specific craft move or a reading strategy that fits with your unit. Over time, you can return to it again and again across various workshops. A read-aloud that is used as a mentor text will become a frequent friend to your students.

If read-alouds help our students learn how to think, talk, and write about texts, then we should make sure our read-aloud choices are varied. Keep a list to track the read-alouds you share and be sure to include a wide variety of authors and genres as well as ways you might use the books with your students. Keeping a sticky note on the inside cover of favorite books can remind you of possible ways you might use them as mentor texts (**Figure 3.3**). Brenda's tried-and-true read-alouds are often tagged in numerous places for teaching possibilities, such as word choice, use of punctuation marks, questions to ponder, times to stop and reflect, and more.

Figure 3.3

Notes on the end pages remind teachers of concepts that can be introduced to the readers throughout the book. Here Lynne shows how to study the end papers with her students. ▼

The sticky note reminds us that author's point of view can be taught using the specific text on this page of informational text. ▼

Figure 3.4

Home–School Connections: Tips for Caregivers When Reading Aloud

- Ask your child for his/her opinion of the book you are sharing.

- Read the book to yourself before you read it aloud with your child (helps with fluency and you can determine if this book is a good match for your child's interests).

- Share the read-aloud (your child reads as one character and you another).

- Be dramatic—ham it up and take on different voices for the characters.

- Create a book basket for each family member to hold their own personal book choices that reflect their interests and passions for read-alouds. (Books can be read more than once!)

What Is a Reading Workshop?

The memories of cooking for my young and growing family remind me of a strong reading workshop. Naturally, I cooked healthy meals on a daily basis, keeping in mind the importance of balancing protein, vegetables, and energy-rich foods that would, in time, make them healthy and strong. During reading workshop, my students get just enough of each essential element: read-aloud, explicit instruction, guided and independent practice, sharing, peer/teacher conferring, assessment, and plenty of time to read. When it came to my family, love was the driving force behind all the meal planning, cooking, and serving meals so we could enjoy them together around our table. When I care deeply for my students, when they feel the warm and inviting tone I purposefully set, strong and trusting bonds are forged. In the end, reading workshop becomes the life-giving, capacity-building experience it is meant to be.

Catherine Gehman,
Grade 4 teacher, Boyertown Area School District

The Extended Benefits of Read-Aloud Time

Sometimes, a read-aloud is just a read-aloud! There are times that all you will do is read aloud and let the magic of the words tumble over and through your students. But whether we're simply enjoying the language of a new book together or digging into it to focus on an instructional goal, our read-alouds and selected mentor texts help children who are readers become students who are writers. Over time, our communities come to know these texts as friends who can help lift the level of their reading and writing.

Though read-alouds are not always used for instructional purposes, they indirectly build interest in new genres and authors, help students discover interesting words, and help young writers become familiar with sentence patterns and ways that authors organize words in their

sentences. And, as students share their thinking about read-aloud texts through writing, they engage in many different forms of writing including book reviews, book talks, character sketches, poems, plays, literary essays, and research projects.

Reading aloud to students on a regular basis, no matter when it's done, is also an effective way of modeling what a fluent reader looks like, sounds like, and feels like during the reading act. As teacher readers, we display our emotions—that we can be moved by an author's words. Just by listening to the rhythm of the words that authors create with sentences, stanzas, and paragraphs, during read-aloud, student writers develop a sense of sentence fluency.

Read-alouds can help students build background knowledge as well. By choosing books with diverse settings and characters, we help students learn about people and places they might not encounter every day. The well-chosen read-aloud can offer opportunities for students to develop empathy and compassion. These books can help classrooms make connections to cultures they may be studying in Social Studies class or perhaps time periods they will study in History. Choosing nonfiction read-alouds will bring greater understanding to current events. It helps students to build background knowledge and helps them make more informed opinions about topics.

Figure 3.5 Brenda and her students share their thinking about a read aloud in small group discussions.

Texts with rich vocabulary and varied sentence structures help readers develop an ear for language—the rhythms and structures—and how authors place perfect words in perfect places. Using the read-aloud for vocabulary study can provide opportunities for the entire class to create word walls that highlight interesting words and inspire young writers to try new words for "tired" words. Splash favorite sentences from favorite read-alouds around the room to showcase figurative language and unusual sentence structures.

The read-aloud also helps teachers work with their students to practice and internalize skills such as making predictions, visualizing words and sentences, and drawing conclusions, to name a few. Using a section of the read-aloud with a small group allows the group to practice a skill or strategy together and support each other as readers work toward independence. Debbie Miller (2018) reminds us that "the read-aloud is a scaffold for children's independent thinking. During work time, children practice what they've learned about reading and thinking during read-aloud and transfer it to their independent reading" (43). Used this way, the read-aloud offers our readers a model they can use as they work independently during their workshop time.

Interactive Read-Aloud

Whereas traditional read-alouds tend to position the teacher as the reader, interactive read-alouds give students opportunities to try out different participatory roles by listening to the text, talking about it, and extending thinking through writing. This can look like students sharing with a partner, a triad, or another version of a small group. Students often gather on a carpet, facing the teacher in an area with a chart stand to record the group's thinking, or sit on chairs or carpet pieces in a semicircle. The students should make sure there is room for them to turn and talk with their partner. Assigning a partner is one way to make sure that students know who to talk with to share their thinking. This practice saves valuable time each day! What is important to note here is that the texts being used for interactive read-alouds are often beyond the instructional reading

level of most of the children even though they are age and interest level appropriate. We believe this is important, as it gives all students access to books that can make a difference in their lives while learning how to use the nomenclature of readers and writers (academic language) and collectively growing background knowledge as they continue to move through the text. Here are some ways to engage readers during interactive read-aloud time:

- Stop 'n Jot during Read-Aloud. To use this practice, find key locations in the read-aloud ahead of time where you will stop to give students a chance to think, ink, pair, and share. They will need their notebooks and pencils as they gather on the rug. Sometimes, students bring a clipboard as well to make it easier to write. When it's time to stop and jot, students can offer a response to the text, ask a question, make a prediction or an inference, notice the author's craft, or even draw a quick sketch of what they are seeing in their mind. These jots can also be shared with a partner or as a whole group. Sometimes, you can ask for a specific jot, such as "What do you now know about the main character?"

- Thinking Aloud to Demonstrate Your Reading Process. During interactive read-alouds, we can make our reading process visible to our students by sharing the strategies we use to make meaning of the text. For instance, we may purposefully choose to demonstrate how we infer or how we can ask great questions. We let our students "see" our process as we strive to make meaning from the text. These think-alouds can occur before, during, and/or after reading. For example, before reading Jacqueline Woodson's *The Day You Begin* (2018), we might study the cover and let students know where we think the character is, what she's feeling at that moment, and why we think so. Then, during reading, we might stop to "read" the pictures, reminding students that doing so is an important part of reading a picture book that can reveal a great deal about setting, character, problem, and conflict. Practice ahead of time, marking the spots where you will think aloud.

> **TEACHER TIP:** When assigning sharing partners for interactive read-alouds, consider different partnerships and the purposes they serve. Sometimes you might want to have readers with similar reading interests or levels working together. At other times, you might want to set things up so that certain partners can serve as models for other partners as they get their bearings.

How Do We Choose Read-Alouds?

When you set out to select a read-aloud text to share with your reading community, you have a lot to consider. Will you read chapter books? Picture books? Poetry? Nonfiction? A graphic novel? All of the above or more in one day? Why this book and not that book? Choosing the read-aloud is not a random act. It requires you to consider your purposes and goals the text addresses, as well as the students in your class.

- Will this book be used as a mentor text for reading strategies, writing strategies, or both? Choose a book where you can model a reading strategy or writing strategy and provide opportunities for students to practice it in whole group or with a partner. Look for author's craft, new conventions, and new organizational structures such as flashbacks or seesaw text. Look for global structures and substructures such as cause and effect, time order, or problem/solution in nonfiction texts.

- Will it serve as a way to build background knowledge? The read-aloud can introduce a topic, time period, or experts in the field for science and social studies units. Picture books can be shared to build background knowledge and schema because they create mental images that students carry into the reading of more complex texts.

- Will this book serve to build and sustain your community of readers? Our read-alouds can celebrate the unique qualities of our students. Will it build self-respect and self-worth? Will it help your students value each other and confront their feelings and fears? Reads-alouds can be a way to deliver social-emotional learning in a powerful yet engaging way.

- Does this text help students learn how to navigate a text? For example, when you share a non-narrative informational text, you can notice and discuss nonfiction text features such as sidebars, words in boldface print, and captions.

- Will this book introduce a new organizational structure? For instance, some books use a repeating sentence as a way to lead readers through the story, focusing them on what is important.

- Will this book introduce a new genre? Choosing genres that aren't usually read aloud—modern fairy tales, science fiction, biography, non-narrative nonfiction, mythology, fables, Arthurian tales, graphic novels, to name a few—will help children in our classes broaden their definition of what reading is and see new reading possibilities for themselves.

- Will this book introduce a new author? The read-aloud can invite readers to find new favorite authors. Tried-and-true authors populate our favorite read-aloud lists, but finding a new author allows children to meet new ideas and writing styles. Following blogs like The Nerdy Book Club (https://nerdybookclub.wordpress.com/) is a way to introduce yourself to newer authors and books.

- Will this book validate readers' perspectives of themselves and promote empathy and compassion for others? As Rudine Sims Bishop (1990) reminds us, literature can offer mirrors where children see themselves and their own experiences or windows into a new world and life experiences for our class community, as it "transforms human experience and reflects it back to us, and in that reflection, we can see our own lives and experiences as part of the larger human experience" (ix).

Video 3.1 ▶

Why We Read Poetry

Poet **Janet Wong** provides a rationale to read poetry every day.

Finally, one terrific but often overlooked source of read-aloud texts features works from the students in our classrooms. Finding texts that our students have written that can be shared creates a space in our community that says, "You are a writer. Your words have value." When we use our students' writing as the read-aloud, we create mentors and experts in our classroom. Children become teachers.

> **TEACHER TIP:** Use poetry! "Poems are the great equalizer for both reading and writing" (Dorfman and Cappelli 2012, 2). Because poems are often short text, they invite us to reread and revisit them often. Consider using a poem to teach vocabulary, word choice, mood, tone, grammar, punctuation usage, comprehension skills (e.g., opinion, facts, drawing conclusions, main ideas, inferring), and oral reading practice.

Final Thoughts

The read-aloud is a treasured time in many classrooms. It is a valuable time for our growing readers and for our community. A time to create not only a place for reading, but also a space for modeling what a fluent reader looks like and sounds like. Reading aloud offers opportunities to expand young readers' vocabulary, grow their comprehension skills, introduce new genres, engage in community discussions, and see the possibilities for what literate lives entail. With read-alouds strongly in place, children see reading as something that is pleasurable and desirable—something they want to do for their entire lifetime.

CHAPTER 3: *The Power of Read-Alouds and Mentor Texts to Inspire* | **43**
Community and Support the Reading Workshop

Figure 3.6 Teachers and students find joy when sharing favorite books together each day. Sharing books brings everyone together as one community.

Stop and Reflect

1. What practices could you try in order to maximize your read-aloud time? Perhaps you could start your day with your read-aloud. What about assigning "talking partners" and areas where students can find a seat quickly to save some time?

2. Examine the texts you use as read-alouds. Do they show a variety of perspectives? Can your students see themselves reflected in the characters featured in the texts you choose? It's important for all students to see themselves in the pages of a book. Are you making diverse and equitable choices in the literature you use in your read-aloud?

Something to Try

Examine your read-alouds. Try a new author or a new genre that will foster new ways of thinking and/or help your students take risks as readers and writers. Include interesting nonfiction texts to demonstrate how a reader can dip in and out of the text, depending on their interests and needs. Consider picture books. They appeal to a wide range of age levels, use wonderful words, and have appealing illustrations. Poems can be terrific sources for quick, high-interest read-aloud experiences. Consider starting the day with a poem and think about the way each poem can build and sustain your reading community.

Chapter 4

Responding to Reading

Writing about reading can deepen the reading experience. It should not be done with every text a student reads or every time a student reads during independent reading, but used wisely and with exceedingly good judgment, it can truly enhance a child's experience with text.

– Pam Allyn and Ernest Morrell,
Every Child a Super Reader

Hailey walks up to Brenda, looking around to see if anyone else notices. She holds her independent reading book tightly. She knows she has to wait for Brenda to finish her conference, and she really shouldn't be standing there, waiting. But she just can't help herself. Brenda finishes up with her conference and sends the student on his way. Hailey rushes to her side. Before Brenda can say a word, Hailey gushes, "Mrs. K, you aren't going to believe this!" Her eyes are filled with unbelief as she continues. "The grandmother is deathly sick!" At this, she stops and looks around to see if anyone else is listening. Brenda nods. She knows the book but wants Hailey to continue. "She has . . ." and here she pauses and whispers, so no one will hear, "p-new-mia! It's deadly for old people!"

"Oh no!" Brenda replies—but doesn't correct her yet. She'll tell her the word is pneumonia later; for now all Hailey wants is an acknowledgment that this is a predicament for the main character.

"Yes, this could change everything!" Hailey says. "I have to find out what happens, but I needed to tell someone."

She walks away, reading as she goes.

Reading workshop offers a space for students to fully step into themselves as readers. As educators, we are devoted to cultivating a love of reading in our students. We love to read and want to develop students who are lifelong readers, too. Like Hailey, readers want and need to respond to what they've read. A text to a friend about a book. A conversation with colleagues in a book club. A quick jot of favorite lines from a memorable text in a journal. A rating on GoodReads. Or, a satisfied sigh as they finish reading something they've been savoring. Readers want and need to respond. Response is part of leading a readerly life.

Most of the work of a reader is done silently, invisibly, in the mind of the reader. Conversation allows us to see what a reader is thinking and doing as they read, helping us access their thoughts. By having conversations throughout the reading of a text, we can engage and encourage children to think in new ways as they read. At times, we will want to slow down the reader and encourage a written response that the reader can reread and reflect upon, and then revise their thinking and understanding.

What Is the Importance of Reader Response?

Reading workshop helps teachers foster a spirit of curiosity and appreciation of literature. To make this happen, many opportunities for students' voices to be heard should occur on a daily basis. Every student brings unique experiences, abilities, and interests to the literature and informational texts they read. Reading should invite sharing, and to that end, oral and written response during independent reading can validate each student's role in reading workshop and open the door to new understandings as they voice their reactions and support their thinking and feelings by returning to the text. Rosenblatt's transactional theory of reader response (1978, 1982) supports the practice of expression of personal thoughts and feelings, real-life connections, and individualized meaning-making responses with the text on hand.

Personal response is the first thing readers do. They connect to the book they are reading on some level. Personal response allows the reader to re-evaluate their life through the experience of a text. Sometimes, this kind of response isn't necessarily shared with anyone. The reader pauses to think about the text and make a connection. These responses can be text-to-self, text-to-text, or text-to-world (Keene and Zimmerman 1997). Text-to-self connections are personal connections that a reader makes between a text and their own experiences or life. Reading comes alive when a text-to-self connection is made, such as, "This story reminds me of the time my grandfather taught me how to overcome my fear and learn to swim at Lake Wallenpaupack."

Soon, as readers develop a collection of books they have read, they are able to make connections to other texts they've experienced. Often, they can make connections with books by the same author, reading material from the same genre, or books written on the same subject matter. These connections are called text-to-text connections. Readers acquire insight during reading by thinking about how the ideas and events from their current read connect to other texts they remember. "I also remember reading about jellyfish as one of the world's most dangerous animals in a book by Melissa Stewart" would be an example of a text-to-text connection.

Text-to-world connections are the bigger connections that a reader brings from background knowledge or schema. Readers often rely on prior knowledge and experience to help them understand what they are reading and use that knowledge to make connections. We all have ideas about how the world works that go far beyond our own personal experiences. We learn so much about things through television, movies, and social media. Teachers try to use text-to-world connections when they teach lessons in science, social studies, and literature. An example of a text-to-world question might be *How are events in this story similar to or different from things that happen in our community?* When you teach students how to connect to text, they are able to better understand what they are reading (Harvey and Goudvis 2000). Dipping into prior knowledge and experiences is a good starting place when teaching strategies because every student has unique situations, knowledge, opinions, and emotions that they can draw upon.

Readers respond to a text in several ways. Shared responses are essential to help build the common literary ground that binds a community of readers together. Readers learn as they listen to the responses of other readers. Response helps teachers make judgments and predictions about their students' reading process. Carol Brennan Jenkins (1999), reading specialist and teacher educator, discusses reader response as critical, aesthetic/personal, and biographical response. Critical response offers an analysis or synthesis of a text. It considers the reader's reactions to literature as essential to interpreting the meaning of the text. Here, it is important to examine the author's writing style—the word choice and the craft (imagery, voice, tone, and mood that is created). A student may think about, write about, or talk about responses to questions such as:

- What did you notice about the author's style?
- How did the author create a mood?
- What did you notice about the author's choice of words (verbs, adjectives, proper nouns, etc.)?
- Does the author do something that is unique or unusual? What is it?

Biographical response helps students to connect with the authors. Students examine the text through the lens of the author's life. Response can center around one or several of the following questions:

- Why did the author write this book?
- Do you think one of the characters really was the author? Explain.
- How was the author's life similar to this story? (Read the "Author's Note" or "About the Author" or look up the author's website.)
- How is your life similar to the life of one of the characters in this story?

Reader response keeps readers engaged and focused on the text. According to Cris Tovani (2000), reader response is a way to make sure your readers are actively participating. It helps readers get a clearer picture of what is happening in the text, remember what they have read, and ask questions. It helps them to stop and think about what the characters are feeling and the motivation behind their actions. It helps readers think about the impact of the information they're gathering from the text.

The Types of Reader Response

Encouraging our readers to respond to what they are reading in varied formats allows all members of the reading community to participate. Many students can begin by engaging in conversations with a partner or small group. Some students need more time to listen actively and may not always vocalize their thinking. Written responses in a reader's notebook or book log can help students make their thinking visible and permanent while fostering revision possibilities. Reader response opportunities help to grow a reader's identity, fostering the conscious notion of "I am a reader" in all reading workshop community members.

CONVERSATIONS

As readers engage with books that impact their thinking, conversations allow readers to express their thoughts and opinions, as well as question the text. Readerly conversations are not limited to the completion of a text. In a community of readers (see **Chapter 2**), children are safe to express their thoughts and questions with their peers and their teacher throughout the reading of a text. Readers might challenge a character's actions, confront an opinion with an opposing view, or ask questions for clarification. Responding through talk allows many readers to participate and many thoughts to be shared. This allows readers to learn from and with peers, increasing engagement and understanding.

Lively conversations around a book can be planned (e.g., stopping at a specific spot in a read-aloud) or spontaneous. They can be teacher generated or student initiated. They can be led with the whole class, a book club, or with one trusted friend. Dorothy Barnhouse and Vicki Vinton (2012), literacy consultants for schools across the United States, caution teachers that, when engaging in conversations with students, they should "refrain from dangling our own understanding of a text in front of students" (7) because we want children to construct their own interpretation and thinking about a text, not ours. In this way, response conversations become authentic.

Keep in mind that silence is also an acceptable way to respond to a text. As an adult, we may not need to say anything to indicate how much a text has meant to us. We may sigh, place the book prominently on our shelf, or just hold the ending in our hearts. Do we allow the readers in our class the same opportunity? Silence in a discussion does not always signal a deficit in thinking but rather a need to sit longer with the information, considering its implications, before moving on or engaging in conversation. Slowing down the response so more time can be spent on considering the meaning of the text can be done via written responses in readers' notebooks (see **Figure 4.1**).

Figure 4.1 A student uses her notebook to explore character traits through drawings and labels and then expands her thinking through written response.

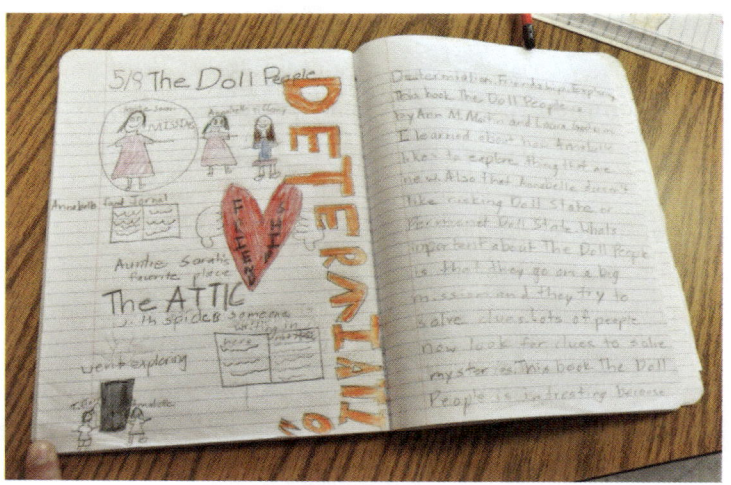

WRITTEN RESPONSE: THE READER'S NOTEBOOK

During reading workshop, the reader's notebook is a perfect place to collect responses in writing and can offer us a glimpse into the thinking a child is doing while reading. As readers use their notebooks to expand their initial sticky-note thinking and write to think through a comment or section of text, we are able to peer into their minds and watch them wrestle with ideas and use strategies to make meaning (see **Figure 4.2**). In *Notebook Connections* (2009), Aimee Buckner describes notebooks as "the place for [students] to document their thinking and growth, to support their ideas for group discussion, and to explore their own thoughts about a text without every entry being a judgment of their reading progress" (6).

Whether you call them notebooks or journals, keeping notes in a particular place provides students with a tool that encourages thinking, requiring our readers to slow down, reflect on their reading, use strategies they've been taught, and engage with the text in a way that makes sense for the reader. Readers' notebooks provide the freedom for students to record their wonderings while taking reading to a new level—an active process of personal meaning-making. In some instances, you might choose to expand written response options to dialogue journals, where teachers write back to their students about their responses. You can make slight adjustments in this practice by inviting students to write their dialogue journal responses as letters to their thinking partners. Then, instead of responding to the letters in written form, students can trade journals when they come to circle, read their partners' letters silently, and respond to them through oral response. This adjustment can cut back on the amount of writing required of dialogue journals but still be an effective means of capturing reader response while linking writing to the reading process and inviting deeper conversations.

Figure 4.2

Possible Responses for a Reader's Notebook

- Questions or observations about characters, plot, theme, and author's style
- Reading Plans: Titles of books to read, authors to study
- Powerful lines that might spark writing and thinking
- Powerful leads and powerful endings
- Quotes from authors, student writing, peers
- Discussions with self to clarify and identify areas of confusion
- Interesting words to explore as self-selected vocabulary
- Concept maps, story maps, lists, graphic organizers, drawings
- Questions leading to research possibilities (nonfiction)
- Examples of literary devices and imagery from mentor texts: mood, symbolism, foreshadowing, irony, etc.

To get started with notebooks, introduce them and their uses through a procedural minilesson. Imagine bringing in your own notebook to share with your class, showing them the different ways you have used your reader's notebook to think through books you are reading and to reflect on what you have read. Revisit entries and talk about what you wrote or drew, why the entry was significant, and how this helped you make meaning as you read. Your example helps children understand the importance of keeping the notebook and creates excitement for starting this new tool. Creating an anchor chart with some guidelines for response can be an effective way to encourage a wide variety of responses (see **Figure 4.3**). Of course, we always invite students to move beyond guidelines and discover new ways to respond to texts, discovering their unique response styles on their personal journeys through the literature they read.

Figure 4.3

Guidelines for Readers' Notebooks

- Take time to write down your thinking while you are reading–your feelings, thoughts, reactions, and opinions.
- Date your entry and, if possible, write down the page number from the book in case you want to return to it to share or verify your thoughts.
- Ask questions about the characters–their behaviors and motives–and about the plot as it unfolds.
- Write about what surprises or confuses you.
- Write your opinion of the book–praise or criticize.
- Make predictions about what will happen next as you are reading. Don't forget to change those predictions as you read.
- Are the characters making good decisions? Do you approve of their actions/decisions?
- Make a connection with your own experiences and share similar experiences from your life or from other books you have read.
- Try to do your best with spelling and to write in sentences, but journals will not be graded. So long as you respond with your ideas, thoughts, and feelings on a regular basis (does not have to be daily), you will receive full credit for your efforts.
- Be careful not to stop to write too often, only when it is something you want to think about later or as a way to clarify your understanding.

TEACHER TIP: A reader's notebook can be as unique as the reader. Decide if students will use notebooks they purchase individually or if everyone will use something similar. Notebooks can be decorated to show a reader's interests, books they love, or reading goals. We prefer bound notebooks for students, so pages don't get torn out.

BOOK LOGS

A book log is a tool used to document the books students have read during reading workshop and outside of school. In its simplest form, the log includes titles and, possibly, a quick rating. Most book logs allow students to date their entries, include the authors and genres, and then give the books reaction ratings: 5–1 stars, thumbs up/thumbs down, happy/sad face, and the like. Other logs allow children to include the date each title was started and when it was completed. As adult readers, we may keep some sort of log, especially if we read a lot and want to recall what we've read and enjoyed. Many adults keep Goodreads accounts so they can log what they're currently reading, what they want to read, and what they've read previously (with a star rating system as well as a place to comment).

Children who keep logs and use them to reflect on their reading see themselves as readers. In *The CAFE Book: Engaging All Students in Daily Literacy Assessment* (2019), Gail Boushey and Joan Moser talk about the importance of helping students establish a reading identity. They can see how many books they have read and the genres they seem to gravitate to or avoid. Using a log this way allows our readers to set goals for increasing their amount of reading as well as discover new genres. When book logs are used to simply document a child's reading life, rather than as a form of assessment or to win a "reading prize," this tool can help a young reader grow their reading identity and offer them proof that they indeed are readers. In this way a log allows readers to make a response. Our readers need to have a vision for where they are heading, working to set doable goals, and imagining where they want to be as readers by the end of the school year.

Figure 4.4 A book log builds reading identity by reminding students of what they read during a given time. When students reflect on their logs, they note what kinds of books they read and may set a goal to try out a new genre, author, or topics to read about.

Name _____

#	Title	Author	S	F	Rating
1	The Doll People	Martin & Goodwin	Nov 15	Nov 25	★ ★ ★ ★ ★ *Circle your rating*
2	Fairy Tale Detectives (Sisters Grimm 1)	Michael Buckley	Nov 26		★ ★ ★ ★ ★ *Circle your rating*

When Is It Time to Shift to Response?

The work of a reader during reading workshop is to read. We believe children need to spend the majority of their independent reading time READING! But we know responding to what they read at the most appropriate times helps readers make meaning, thinking about what they will encounter as they read and as they continue to read their books. With this in mind, we make room across the act of reading for students to stop, reflect, and respond as needed.

RESPONDING BEFORE READING

As readers, we implicitly respond and think before we read. We consider what we know about the genre, the book series, or perhaps the author. We may read the book jacket to gather insights and clues about the plot and characters, or perhaps conduct some research to gather information about the topic from other sources. Consider the readers in your classroom. Primary children often preview the text by doing "picture walks" with the teacher and/or peers. In a picture walk, children go page by page, orally predicting what they will read about or learn. This, in its own way, is an act of responding to the text. As the child and teacher do this together, the teacher can highlight key words and vocabulary the young reader will encounter in the conversation. This strategy builds vocabulary and excitement for reading the text.

Activating prior knowledge, building concepts, making predictions, focusing attention, and arousing interest before reading leads readers to a richer understanding of the text and greater engagement. We can ask students to discuss or record their before-reading thoughts. The reader's notebook is a great place to house initial thinking because readers can return to early entities and confirm or revise their thinking as they gather more information while reading. Using simple sentence starters (see **Figure 4.5**) can help readers gather their thoughts and questions before they begin a new book.

Figure 4.5

Sentence Starters for Before Reading Responses

- I think this book will be about . . . because . . .
- I really want to read this book because . . .
- I know . . . about the topic and hope to learn . . .
- I choose to read this book because . . .
- I am wondering . . .

RESPONDING DURING READING

During reading, students continue to engage in personal meaning-making strategies. These strategies include monitoring for understanding. Usually, this response is essential in the early stages of a book where meaning is being constructed, clarified, and/or affirmed. Other meaning-making strategies include making inferences and drawing conclusions. Students can use sentence stems to help them with this kind of response.

- I think the main character is feeling _____ because . . .
- It sounds like . . .

- She probably will _____ because . . .
- I am learning . . .
- The most important ideas in this book/article are . . .

During reading is also the time that readers will continue to make predictions and find information in the text to confirm those predictions, evolve them, or make entirely new ones. Making predictions during reading is an attempt to speculate about what is going to happen as the plot develops and synthesize clues to validate or invalidate those predictions. During reading time is a perfect place to grow wonder and reflect on what is going on, what the "inside story" is, or what confusion is arising as the student works hard to comprehend the text.

As they read, a student can collect vocabulary words they find interesting, or want to know about in their reader's notebook. They can copy the sentence containing the word they want to explore to help them understand it in the context in which it was used. Then they can use their notebook to help them make the word a part of their everyday vocabulary by creating a drawing, finding antonyms and synonyms, using the word in a sentence they created, or defining the word in language they would use. Often, teachers ask students to create a special section in the readers' notebook for self-selected vocabulary that can become a great bridge between reading and writing workshop, too!

TEACHER TIP: Intrinsically motivated readers read because it gives them enjoyment or satisfaction in some way. We need to find ways to motivate our students to read other than contests, prizes, and pizza parties. Giving children our full attention as they respond is all they need to feel affirmed and motivated to read.

RESPONDING AFTER READING

When a book has made an impact on you as a reader, you want to respond. Offer children opportunities to share their excitement of reading with peers through book talks (see **Chapter 6**), chatting with you about the book, introducing it to a partner, discussing it with their book club, or simply savoring it. These responses can be oral or written. Here is an opportunity for you to respond as well, by redirecting, expanding, and/or refocusing readers' comments. These comments are often in the form of suggestions that can lead readers to add to their thinking about a text, nudging them in directions they may not have explored on their own.

Do you remember book reports and those dreaded dioramas we were required to complete after reading a book in elementary school? As a parent, Sunday evenings were a nightmare when a book report was due. Even the act of recording a paragraph after completing every book read can become burdensome. Consider carefully what you ask children to do in response to reading. And remember, not every book needs a response and not every response needs a directive from you. **Figure 4.6** showcases some ideas to get you and your readers started.

Figure 4.6

After-Reading Response Possibilities

1. Praise or criticize a book, author, or author's style.
2. Write on a sticky note or record a book recommendation and place it on the inside cover of the book.
3. Share similar moments in your life that relate to the characters or plot from the book you just read.
4. Share similar moments/experiences/situations/information in other books you've read to the book you completed.
5. Encourage students to add their thoughts to a graffiti board (a shared writing space where students record their comments, questions, and reactions to a topic/book).
6. Reflect in your reader's notebook on ideas offered during a reading conversation or end-of-workshop reflection by your community members.
7. Add to your reading log and consider next steps. What will you read next?

8   Start a book club/literature circle/partnership to share a book you treasure and want to reread with peers.

9   Create an electronic comment board to share your thoughts.

10   Laugh, cry, sigh.

Final Thoughts

Readers want to respond to books that are impactful. They have a desire to share the joy and wonder discovered in a good book with other readers. As adults we do this naturally—texts, social media, book log sites, book clubs. A student reader is part of the classroom community. Students should understand that they are not alone and that reading is not a solitary act. In our classrooms we have the opportunity to create an environment where responding to a book is natural and desirable. There is no limit to the types of responses your students can share. Encourage sincere, honest responses where readers share their thoughts, feelings, likes, opinions, and insights. It is important that students believe they have the freedom to respond to texts that reflect their individuality and their reading tastes. To view themselves as readers, our students will need opportunities to collaborate, share their reading discoveries, choose their own paths, and reflect on what they are learning about themselves as readers.

Stop and Reflect

1. How can you create space in your schedule to allow students to chat about their reading?

2. How can you challenge your readers to explore and expand the potential for personal response through their readers' notebooks?

Something to Try

Keep a reader's notebook for your own reading. Use it in the same ways your students might use theirs, perhaps recording passages and reflecting on what they mean to you or keeping a page of new vocabulary words. Share your notebook with students along with your thinking about how you decided what to include in it and how doing so has helped you reflect on yourself as a reader and your reading habits.

Chapter 5

Minilessons: Bringing Readers Together for Explicit Instruction

The minilesson helps students to build a repertoire of different strategies they will use at an appropriate time while independently reading.

– Jennifer Serravallo,
The Reading Strategies Book: Your Everything Guide to Developing Skilled Readers

The children have gathered on the carpet. They are sitting next to their reading partners. They know what to expect—Mrs. M. will model a reading strategy or ask them to consider a new line of thinking, they will try this out with their partner, and then they will work on it by themselves before moving on to independent reading time. The routine is comfortable and keeps them focused.

"Readers, have you ever chosen a book that you just don't want to read? You've been working at it for a while and you just don't want to read it anymore. Is there a time when it is okay to abandon a book—even if your goal is to stay with a book?" Heads nod. "I know I have had that experience. I'm wondering if we can decide together, when is it okay to abandon a book?"

With the expectation set, children turn to partners to begin discussing their thinking about abandoning a book. They take brief notes, express their ideas freely, coming up with what they think will be a good list to share with their community. Mrs. M. listens in on conversations.

After a few minutes, she calls the children together. "So, what have you decided?" Children are eager to share their thoughts. Mrs. M. grabs a marker and begins creating an anchor chart: "Reasons to Abandon a Book." Jason suggests, "The book topic is not something I am interested in and I get really confused." The class agrees to add this to the chart. The conversation continues as the group discusses each suggestion before deciding whether to add it to the chart or not.

"So, I think we have decided that there are times to abandon a book." She points to the chart. "Let's try this list out for a few days and see how it works. If you decide to abandon a book, jot down why you are abandoning it so we can talk about it."

The lesson concludes and readers are off to read their independent book choices—minilesson complete for today, in twelve minutes.

What Is a Minilesson?

The minilesson is the time and place in the workshop for explicit instruction, when the teacher and the students gather to learn together as a community of readers. It's an intentional part of the workshop where the teacher considers all the readers in the community and decides what lessons, skills, strategies, or procedures this particular group needs at this point in time. It is a time for the class to engage in a practice that will move the community forward as readers. In the Fountas and Pinnell Literacy™ Blog (2019), the authors describe reading minilessons as "concise, explicit lessons with a purposeful application in building your students' independent reading competencies."

Thoughtful workshop teachers plan minilessons with the readers and the community in mind, determining what they need and then considering how to model and demonstrate the goal students need to engage in independently. Minilessons serve different purposes and vary in timing. Some lessons are about ten minutes long, while others may take longer, especially when introducing a new concept. The goal, however, is to always keep in mind who is doing the work and build in time to practice the concept introduced through the lesson during guided practice and

independent reading time. Instruction centers on moving readers toward greater independence as soon as possible.

THE GRADUAL RELEASE OF RESPONSIBILITY MODEL

Figure 5.1 The gradual release model shows how responsibility and ownership moves from teacher control to student control. In a minilesson, the teacher initially is the expert who delivers explicit instruction to the whole group. From there we move to guided practice ("we do") where students try out the new learning under the close observation of the teacher. This can include collaborative practice with a partner or individual as students try it out and share with the whole group. Finally, we come to independent practice where students act alone to use the new learning and reflect their understanding.

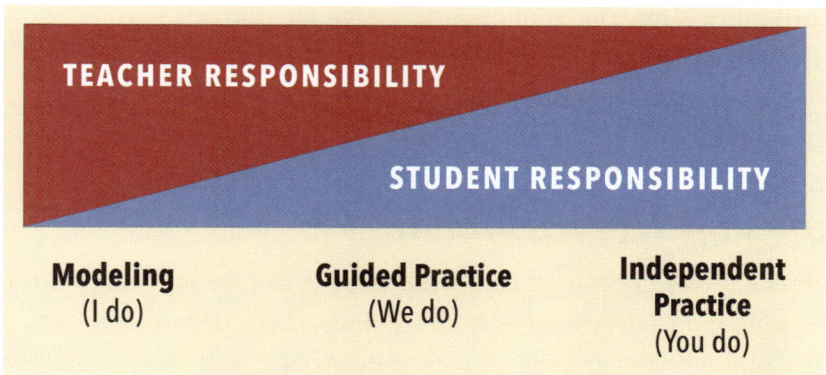

As more schools shift to a responsive workshop model that employs the gradual release of responsibility for classroom instruction, it's invaluable to have a practical and easy-to-follow minilesson format to use in planning (see **Figure 5.1**). In today's classroom, there's wide support for modeling instruction with an emphasis on guiding students through a gradual release of responsibility (Fisher and Frey 2013; Pearson and Gallagher 1983; Webb et al. 2019). This model is based on the work of Lev Vygotsky (1978) and his Zone of Proximal Development (the difference between what a learner can do with help and what the learner can do without help) as well as the instructional scaffolding work of Pearson and Gallagher (1983).

Routman (2018) discusses a similar model, the optimal learning model, in *Literacy Essentials: Engagement, Excellence, and Equity for* All *Learners.* The difference between Routman's model and the traditional gradual release model is the focus. In the optimal learning model, the focus is on allowing students to take charge of their learning as early as possible in the process. The importance of giving students more responsibility for learning a skill or strategy early on is that it helps them gain confidence and self-esteem as readers. This scaffold for instruction is anchored in the important idea of purposeful planning, allowing teachers to decide how much modeling, practice, and support is needed before readers can effectively apply the concept introduced in the minilesson.

As you continue through this chapter and reflect on the minilesson portion of the workshop model, carefully consider the role shared responsibility plays. The minilesson is a time for students to try out the new learning and for the teacher to observe, monitor, and make adjustments before releasing students to try the new learning independently.

Types of Minilessons

Minilessons vary in content. Some minilessons will focus on the *procedures* of the workshop. These lessons help students gain independence in how the workshop moves and the readers' responsibilities in the ongoing work of the workshop. For example, a procedural minilesson could be designed to help students locate resources and materials quickly during the reading workshop. Minilessons can also concentrate on areas such as *responding to reading through writing* (e.g., written character analysis) or focusing on *skills or strategies* that will help readers make meaning (e.g., phonics skills or comprehension strategies). Topics will vary, time will vary, and the type of minilesson used will vary, but all lessons will contain the same basic structure that includes: a "hook," explicit instruction such as naming and demonstrating the skill or strategy being taught, and time to practice through application (see **Appendix D: Minilesson Template and Samples**). The minilesson is the teaching moment in our workshop.

PROCEDURAL MINILESSONS

Procedural lessons are lessons that focus on the logistical aspects of the workshop (see **Figure 5.2**). At the start of the school year, time spent on procedural lessons will help ensure that the workshop runs smoothly later. What does a reading workshop look like, sound like, feel like? How do readers select books, and when? How is a reader's notebook set up? When do we use our notebooks? Where do we store our materials and how do we get them? Where do we sit for the minilesson? Taking the time to discuss the need for procedures and then teaching students how to do them allows us to streamline the workshop process and spend more time actually doing the work of the workshop—reading. Procedural lessons are also sprinkled into the workshop throughout the year as the attuned teacher notices a need to refine a procedure, reteach a procedure, or introduce a new procedure to the community. These procedures become the routines of the workshop and will save you valuable time. Consider your goal as you visualize your workshop. What will it take to make that picture your reality? Jot down some lessons you will need to teach to make this happen in your classroom.

Video 5.1

Procedural Minilesson
First graders revisit workshop procedures with a minilesson on best places to sit.

Figure 5.2

Procedural Minilesson Possibilities

- Conducting effective discussions or having a "real" conversation
- When and how to abandon a book
- Different ways to respond to fiction/nonfiction during literature circle/book club work
- What to do if a passage is confusing and you need help
- How to use the classroom library effectively and care for books
- Ways to find a partner or create a book club around a book or author
- What you need to be ready for a conference
- Ways to practice reading; multiple ways to read and reread a book (primary)
- Asking for help when the teacher is working with others
- How to "read" the room (primary)

RESPONSE MINILESSONS

A reading journal or notebook can help your students develop their ability to reflect and wonder, putting their thoughts and feelings into words on a page. In this way, students can document how they are growing and changing as readers. Responding to a text in a written format helps students begin to understand that a reader's abilities vary with the text they are reading. Students begin to see their reading development as an ongoing process. Sometimes, a reading journal entry can present as a metacognitive conversation, where readers "talk to the text" or "question the author" to deepen their understanding of the text, clear up confusion, and reflect on their own reading processes. When readers who regularly journal engage in a close read of the text, they often do so with a pencil in hand.

In this kind of minilesson, the goal is to help students understand their reading processes and give them a space to think and write about the text in new ways (see **Figure 5.3**). When students write about their reading, they can gather their thoughts for classroom discussions and small group work, clarify and confirm their thinking, and consider how their thinking has changed. By making their thinking visible, students have the opportunity to consider revision possibilities and reach new understandings of the text and of themselves as readers. A written response gives readers an intimate record of their personal reading journey.

Figure 5.3

Response Minilesson Possibilities

- Writing about turning points, lines that have power, images that stick with us, ways the characters are developed, or language that moves us
- Marking texts with different-color sticky notes, highlighter, or colored pencil—each color representing what students are looking for in a read-through
- Using sticky notes to hold our thinking while reading

- Questioning the meaning and significance of a passage
- Writing about structural and inferential levels of meaning
- Analyzing text on a word-by-word, sentence-by-sentence, or paragraph-by-paragraph basis
- Rereading with a new purpose in mind
- Responding to the author's intent or message

In an example of this type of minilesson, Mrs. Gehman's fourth grade class needed a way to efficiently markup nonfiction texts. She gathered the students together to develop a code for common responses and created an anchor chart as a reference to use when reading independently. Mrs. Gehman started with a code she often used: "S" to stand for "Share this with the class." Students added Q for "I have a question about this" and C for "I connect with this." Students practiced using the coding system while reading a nonfiction selection from their anthology with a partner and then reflected together on the effectiveness of the coding system.

MINILESSONS TO EXPLORE SKILLS AND STRATEGIES

As educators we often interchange the terms *skills* and *strategies* when communicating professionally or with parents. Understanding the subtle difference between these two terms and how they are related enables us to assess and instruct students more effectively. Researchers Afflerbach, Pearson, and Paris (2008) describe the difference between skills and strategies as ways "to distinguish automatic processes from deliberately controlled processes." The fluent reader uses a combination of both—automatic application and use of reading skills, and an intentional, deliberate use of reading strategies. The accomplished reader shifts seamlessly between the two when the situation calls for it. Reading *strategies*, then, are deliberate, goal-directed attempts to control and modify the reader's efforts to decode text, understand words, and construct meaning of text (Afflerbach et al. 2008). Strategies are conscious, metacognitive choices taken by the reader toward a reading goal. Sometimes the chosen strategy is effective and sometimes it is not. Fluent readers have many strategies to choose from and can monitor their success or need to change strategies to reach their reading goals. For teachers, "Our role is to teach children many strategies, teach them early, reteach them often, and connect assessment with reteaching" (Afflerbach, et al. 2008).

Reading *skills*, on the other hand, are automatic actions that result in decoding and comprehension with speed, efficiency, and fluency and usually occur without awareness of the components or control involved (Afflerbach et al. 2008). In other words, once a reader has acquired a skill it is performed unconsciously, much like a habit. This automaticity defines it as a skill. ". . . fluent reading skills are more 'advanced' actions than reading strategies because they are faster, more efficient, and require less thinking and social guidance" (369). Skill lessons help students engage with a text to make meaning. They may include lessons on how to infer or predict, how to read with expression, or how to develop a line of thinking.

Continuous instruction of reading strategies and skills using the gradual release of responsibility model affords teachers the opportunity to explain strategies and model not only the automatic process but the thinking that skillful readers do. Explicit instruction and thinking aloud help children understand what they are doing and why it is important as they develop metacognition of strategies and automaticity of skills. As teachers, we need to know what skills are key for comprehending a specific text, and then provide strategies to access the skill we are presenting in a minilesson. For example, when students are tackling a biography or autobiography, they need to recognize what is offered as opinion and what is stated as fact (skill). To support this, we might introduce a strategy to help students identify generalizations that signal an opinion such as "all" or "everyone" or "never." Having children explain their thinking before, during, and after reading helps us assess their acquisition of strategies and usage of skills.

Figure 5.4 Examples of skill and strategy lessons for navigating nonfiction books

Skill Lessons

- Uncovering the meaning of new vocabulary
- Determining the author's purpose
- Determining the author's point of view
- Summarizing vs. retelling
- Determining essential information

Strategy Lessons

- Using transition words and phrases to help determine text structure
- How to read nonfiction–as a "dip in and dip out" process to quickly find the information that you need for research purposes
- Choosing a key term or phrase to be able to collapse a list for summarization purposes
- Ways to self-monitor while you read
- Locating generalizations to be able to determine opinion in nonfiction text

A Planning Format

Planning your minilesson begins with setting an instructional goal. Asking yourself some specific questions is a place to start. *What strategy, skill, response option, or procedure do I want to explicitly teach in this lesson? How will I demonstrate or model this for my students? Will I use a new or previous read-aloud as a mentor text? How will students practice this? How will I support them in their learning?*

Figure 5.5

Components of a Minilesson

- Hook: Purpose
- Explicit instruction: Purpose/model/explain
- Application: Guided practice and independent practice
- Closure
- Sharing and reflection

Most reading workshops follow a common blueprint such as the one shown in **Figure 5.5**. Begin each lesson with a hook; establishing a need for and creating an interest in what is being taught. Ask a question, introduce a new concept, or build on what has been taught. *Readers, yesterday we used characters' words to help us determine a character's traits* . . . Be explicit about the goal of the lesson by naming the concept you will teach. You might say, *Today I want to teach you* . . . Next, model and demonstrate how readers will put it into practice, breaking it down into smaller, bite-sized pieces if necessary. Students observe how the concept works and hear your thinking as you model how you use it in action.

Next, offer students an opportunity to apply the concept, and support them as they do. Working together during guided practice (active engagement) provides students support and allows them to experience success. This guided practice may include a "turn-and-talk," a "think-ink-pair-share," or even a "hand-holding" as you walk through things step by step. During active engagement, students try out the new learning presented in the minilesson with the support of their teacher and peers. It's important to note that not all students will be able to access the concept at the same time or with the same level of understanding, so you'll want to do a quick inventory of who will need more support after the lesson and who will not. This will help you plan for small group instruction and conferences.

As the minilesson ends, remind the children of what was taught and how to use the concept, taking the time to review things as needed and reference the anchor chart that illustrates the work (if one was created). This creates an expectation that the students should try out the new learning on their own during independent reading time. Setting this expectation is key.

As information is taught, readers learn to use it independently in ways that make sense to them. Not every reader will need to follow the step-by-step procedure, nor should they be expected to. When readers begin adapting new learning and finding their own way, they have taken ownership of their reading and are on their way to lifelong reading. We can observe this during independent reading time.

At the close of the workshop, asking children to come together in the instructional area to reflect on the lesson and how they applied the new learning during independent reading will help students set goals and see new possibilities for what has been taught.

Additional Structures to Support Minilessons

At times, you may need to introduce new and sometimes difficult concepts relating to ELA standards and your grade-level curriculum. In these instances, you may need to help students create some "hooks" to attach new knowledge to their existing knowledge. Beginning minilessons from an *inquiry* stance can challenge students' current understandings, maximize the time they spend in instruction, and build their sense of agency. *Frontloading* builds a strong foundation of background knowledge, strategies, and processes to help students tackle the more difficult tasks at hand. *Anchor charts* can help with this by making the community's thinking visible for everyone to see. These visible scaffolds may contain content, strategies, processes, or guidelines that can be used during the learning process or to increase independence during independent reading and written response to reading.

USING INQUIRY IN MINILESSONS

Many of your lessons will begin by explicitly stating the concept you will teach. There are times, however, when you will begin the lesson with a question. For example, you could begin by asking readers a question that will lead to a community discovery: *Readers, I'm wondering if you've ever read a long chapter book and found you were having difficulty carrying information from one chapter to the next. What do you do to remember the important information that will help you build meaning?* This type of approach to the minilesson helps readers create their own understandings of a key issue in your workshop and supports student agency, which gives students voice and choice in their learning, and moves the community forward.

Video 5.2 ▶

Processing Reading Workshop with First Graders Using an Anchor Chart

First grade teacher **Theresa Hunsicker** engages children in thinking about what reading workshop is while creating an anchor chart together.

Peter Johnston, author of *Choice Words: How Our Language Affects Children's Learning* (2004), argues that we want to avoid telling students what to think, instead offering feedback that helps them notice and name problem-solving skills and strategies they are using. Students become agents of their own learning and meaning makers when they are given voice and choice in the classroom.

Beginning your minilesson with a question makes the work relevant, peaks students' curiosity, and challenges students to be thinkers and problem solvers. This inquiry approach places students at the center of spirited discussions, stimulates deep thinking, and fosters engagement rather than compliance. And, in all of this, agency grows—leading to readers that work hard, set higher goals, have greater focus, and stick with learning goals for longer when things get tough (Johnston 2004).

BUILDING A STRONG FOUNDATION WITH FRONTLOADING STRATEGIES

Sometimes, we discover that students have gaps in their understanding and need us to help them access prior knowledge or establish enough background knowledge to understand and be able to apply their new learning. The reality of a complex classroom is that students will have varying amounts of background knowledge on any given topic, strategy, or process. Frontloading activities can vary depending on this reality, ranging from high amounts of background knowledge to almost non-existent, based on the difficulty of the new learning. So, before you teach a minilesson that introduces something new and important, you might try beginning with a frontloading approach. For instance, Brenda is preparing to read aloud a book that takes place in India. She knows that the children in her third grade class have very little background information on the country, its culture, and how some children live in great poverty. She finds kid-friendly videos to share with the class so they will better understand the actions of the main characters in Padma Venkatraman's book *The Bridge Home*.

Figure 5.6

Frontloading Strategies

- Providing multimedia approaches such as videos, photographs, or paintings
- Reading short texts and other alternatives (picture books, poems, essays, articles)
- Performing readers' theater scripts to introduce characters, setting, genre
- Using anticipation and prediction guides
- Thinking aloud to demonstrate your comprehension process
- Inviting guided discussions after exploring information from websites
- Posing thought-provoking questions for quick-write responses
- Providing complementary texts with divergent perspectives, written in varying reading/ grade level abilities to make the content more accessible
- Pre-teaching key vocabulary through visual representations including graphic organizers and sentences where students can use context clues to uncover the word's meaning
- Brainstorming so students can use one another as sources by working collaboratively to pool their shared knowledge

ANCHOR CHARTS SUPPORT TEACHING AND LEARNING

Figure 5.7 Using an anchor chart provides students with a quick reminder and reference to the explicit instruction of the minilesson. Posting the charts where students can have easy access ensures their use.

In our classrooms, anchor charts can support more challenging learning by offering visible records of how we think together as a community of learners for clarity and future reference. These charts (see **Figure 5.8**) can be used to record important ideas shared during the minilesson, during guided practice, and again during the final share and reflection time. Effective anchor charts synthesize thinking and serve as resources students can return to for support over time (Tovani 2011).

TEACHER TIP: Anchor charts as visible representations of students' thinking help not only those students who are contributing to the chart but all students in the class. You can enhance this support feature by:

- Celebrating students' thinking by displaying their names next to the thinking
- Saving time by doing the work of an artist later on, not as part of your minilesson
- Dating and saving anchor charts to serve as tangible artifacts of learning in the classroom
- Taking down anchor charts as new ones are posted to avoid having too many displayed at one time
- Observing how students are using the chart to help them read, write, and talk about the skills, strategies, and key concepts they are learning

Figure 5.8

Examples of Anchor Chart Topics for Reading Workshop

- How to . . . (e.g., retell across your hand [primary], summarize, monitor for meaning)
- Steps to . . . (e.g., infer, determine importance, summarize, envision text)
- Decoding strategies
- Fix-up strategies to help you understand the text
- Making predictions before, during, and after reading
- Understanding what real reading looks like

- Understanding text structures (e.g., cause and effect, problem–solution, chronology, definition/description, compare/contrast)
- How to determine if a book is too easy, too hard, or just right
- What to do when you get stuck on a word
- Book club routines

As you begin planning your anchor charts, consider the purpose of your chart. Are you illustrating your teaching point and what you want students to take with them as they work independently? Will your chart offer steps to follow to access a skill? Is your chart giving information that children will need to strategically move their thinking forward? Does this chart serve to remind students of routines used throughout the workshop? Will you and your students create this chart together, or will the chart be made ahead and uncovered during the teaching session? Remember, the purpose of your chart is to support your teaching and students' reading work.

TEACHER TIP: Primary teachers often rely heavily on visuals to make their charts accessible to all students, which can slow down a minilesson. To save time, consider preparing primary chart graphics in advance and then use a glue stick to add graphics to the chart as components are discussed.

Flexibility with Minilessons

Traditionally, minilessons kick off the reading workshop time. However, the workshop is not a lock-step procedure, and its structure can be adjusted based on the needs of your readers. Consider where your minilesson could land and why. Debbie Miller (2018) reminds us that when planning the workshop, we need to be flexible and adapt our teaching to serve the children in our class and their needs. "As teachers practice, learn, and grow, the structures we use for teaching and learning evolve right along with us. It's not that I'm about reinventing workshop, but I am about flexibility, adaptation, and thinking about workshop (or any structure) in new ways that serve children and put their needs first. I understand now that the workshop structure isn't something we do by heart. Workshops are something we do *with* heart" (54).

Feel free to change things up as needed to support where your readers are in the moment. Maybe your minilesson would work best today after the children have engaged in independent reading. Maybe you'll place it smack in the middle of independent reading time as you notice something that needs to be addressed, or maybe you'll choose not to teach the minilesson at all and, instead, do your teaching as you confer with individual readers and work with small groups.

TEACHER TIP: Most minilessons are not one and done. The power of a minilesson is that it can be revisited, tweaked, and adapted to new situations. Remember, a minilesson is not about mastery but more about approximation and practice, and growth over time. Valuable teaching points can be offered again and again throughout a school year.

What Is Reading Workshop?

Reading workshop is a balanced structured approach to reading instruction that allows for direct and explicit whole group, small group, and individual reading instruction. It allows for students to focus on a short whole-group reading strategy lesson, as well as work on an individual reading goal. It provides students with a significant amount of time to read self-selected just-right books in order to move students into more complex texts, as well as gain a love of reading.

Connie Meyers,
ELA teacher, Souderton Area School District

How Do I Decide What to Teach?

With so many reading goals pulling at our attention, the most important aspect of the minilesson becomes deciding what, exactly, you'll teach. The main way to determine this is to look at the needs of your readers. Assessments should drive our instruction. The daily formative assessments (see **Chapter 10**) teachers use, such as conferences, anecdotal records, reading logs, and journals, provide instructional possibilities. Observations of both written and oral responses during small and whole group instructions, and project-based learning opportunities, help teachers make sound instructional decisions about what to teach and even how to differentiate instruction. Formative assessment measures allow teachers to provide instruction to meet the needs of their unique readers as they develop a deep understanding of their students' reading identities and capabilities. They help teachers make smart decisions and provide opportunities for reteaching throughout the learning process.

Of course, classroom teachers have a responsibility to many stakeholders when deciding what lessons to teach. Minilessons most often arise from local guidelines for grade level curriculum demands, state and national standards, or curriculum mapping that includes a sequence and/or spiraling of skills and strategies to be taught. In addition to being responsible for these standards, teachers are often held accountable to a specific reading series or to units of study purchased by the district. Sometimes, these programs can lead us away from our larger goal—to create lifelong learners. We understand that all of this may seem incongruent with the workshop model; however, there are ways to take the skills and strategies that are indicated in these documents and still have a viable and thriving workshop and reading community. For instance, consider reframing and adapting units you've been given so that they better meet the needs of the children in your classroom. That may include substituting a more contemporary mentor text for one that is presented in the series, or perhaps finding a text that more appropriately reflects the experiences and the cultures of the students sitting before you in this year's class. Think about which mentor texts can best serve your purposes and students and still meet your required goals. You might also consider teaching the skills or strategies presented in your district-provided materials across a variety of minilessons. For example, your reading curriculum may say that your skills focus in a nonfiction unit is summarization, but you know that if you do not first address how to determine what is essential and how to paraphrase, or even how summarization differs from retelling, you cannot teach students how to effectively summarize.

In all of this, prioritize your reading community and the children in it when determining your learning goals as you consider the curriculum. Too often we say things like, "Today I'm teaching main idea and details." But consider the difference if you reworded this statement to something like, "Today I'm helping the readers in my class see how finding a main idea and supporting details will help them better understand nonfiction text." This slight shift in mindset centers our teaching on readers while still honoring the curriculum and standards. It creates an atmosphere where children and their learning become the priority. It allows the teacher to set realistic goals for the readers in the classroom. And it allows teachers to take ownership of their teaching over a mandated program!

Final Thoughts

In the minilesson section of the workshop, teachers create routines that students will eventually take on as their own. Children understand and expect a teaching point, models and demonstrations, and time to practice the concept being taught. The teacher establishes the routines and by internalizing those routines, children are prepared for the learning experience. They are prepared to talk with partners and to engage in the lesson. The routines of the lesson are automatic to students because of procedural lessons and the time they've spent practicing. Readers also understand that, following the minilesson, they will transition to independent reading, moving quickly to a reading spot and beginning to read, because routines of gathering materials and settling in have been taught and practiced as a community.

No one ever said workshop teaching was easy. Decisions abound. Maximizing time in the workshop block begins with deciding how much time to spend on the key components in the workshop; the minilesson, independent reading, share/reflection time. As Regie Routman (2003) reminds us, make every moment of your workshop time count. She suggests we "teach with a sense of urgency," not from a place of anxiety but "mindful of where I need to get them and how little time I have in which to do it." Establishing the routines and creating rituals within the minilesson is the first step toward an environment where this urgent learning can flourish and reading is joyful.

Stop and Reflect

1. Think about your workshop right now. What skills, strategies, responding opportunities, or procedures need to be taught explicitly in the coming weeks? How can this knowledge help you devise a sequence of lessons that prioritize your teaching points.
2. What minilessons have you already taught this year that you'd like to revisit? What adjustments would you make and what effects might those changes cause?

Something to Try

Create a minilesson using the template provided in **Appendix D**. (Remember, this is only one way to plan and organize your thinking). For a start, you might watch the video of a procedural lesson shown on **page 65** and create a plan for a procedural lesson you can try this week.

Chapter 6

Classroom Libraries: Sharing the Excitement of Reading

The book access we offer children in school must be as varied, relevant, current, and engaging as possible. For many children, school offers the only real access opportunities in their lives, so it has to count.

– Donalyn Miller and Colby Sharp,
Game Changer! Book Access for All Kids

Walk into the classroom. Take it all in. The walls, the placement of desks, the seating areas, independent work areas. What grabs your attention? What is the focal point? What stands out? The teacher's work area? The imitation-brick or faux wood-paneled wall? The pretty posters that adorn the classroom walls? Or . . . is it the classroom library and the number of books that fill this space?

The classroom library's placement and arrangement of books throughout the classroom reflects the teacher's intentions, values, and beliefs about reading. In her book *Teaching with Intention* (2008), Debbie Miller suggests that all our teaching decisions begin with our own teaching beliefs, values, and intentions. *How is my classroom library organized and where is it located? Where are all the books—around the room in different areas or only one location? Who takes care of the library? How do children access the library and when? What books will populate this library? What do I hang on the walls surrounding my library—children created, store-bought, filler, or instructional posters?* By reflecting on questions like these you can begin to create and curate a classroom library that reflects the importance of reading and is a living and breathing part of your reading workshop.

Figure 6.1

Easy Access to Classroom Library Books

One middle school teacher, Kristin Haring, uses all her classroom spaces for easy book access and high visibility. In today's world with more social distancing norms, breaking up your classroom library to house your collection makes good sense. Her students at Kutztown Middle School helped her create categories for the many books for reading workshop and book clubs. Kristin regularly applies for grants, including from the Book Love Foundation. She is always looking for the most current reads and ways to purchase multiple copies.

This shelf is often used to display full covers of student picks for "Must Reads!" and a teacher's choice.

Baskets organized by author are placed against the walls and on counter spaces for easy browsing.

Shelves often display categories suggested by students.

Magazines such as *Highlights for Children, National Geographic, Sports Illustrated for Kids, Zoobooks Magazine, Muse Magazine, Kazoo, Illustoria, Ask: Arts and Science for Kids, Cricket,* and *ChopChop* (features kid-friendly and health-conscious recipes) are favorites.

Curating a Library that Lives and Breathes

A library filled with a wide variety of books, media, and genres is an essential component of the reading workshop. In *It's All About the Books: How to Create Bookrooms and Classroom Libraries That Inspire Readers* (2018, 21), authors Landrigan and Mulligan state, "The classroom library is the home of the class' reading community . . . . Its primary role is building a literacy community in each classroom and ensuring that each student is a member" (21).

Figure 6.2 This reader is totally engaged in the reading zone–unaware of anything but what is happening in the pages of a book she chose for independent reading.

Classroom libraries can offer readers books expertly selected by a classroom teacher who has knowledge of curricula and a variety of texts that can supplement and complement what the class is studying. Teachers use their knowledge of students' concerns, needs, and interests to select books that will appeal and be accessible to their readers. They are aware of the range of reading abilities in their reading communities and choose books that span a variety of ability levels to create inviting classroom libraries. They understand that their book collections have the potential to introduce readers to new genres, new topics, new series, new authors, and new book titles that open the world to readers. And they understand that each new school year brings a new group of learners that may have different needs than the previous year's group, so they learn about their students through interest surveys, inventories, conferences, and reader response journals as well as informal observations in order to continually develop classroom libraries that represent their diverse identities and reading tastes.

Figure 6.3

Video 6.1 ▶

Criteria for Classroom Libraries

Past principal and literacy specialist **Gail Ryan** talks to teachers about the classroom library as a place for them to feel at home and choose their own books.

Classroom Libraries are Beneficial to Students in Many Ways; They

- motivate students by encouraging voluntary and recreational reading
- help young people develop an extensive array of literacy strategies and skills
- provide access to a wide range of reading materials that reflect abilities and interests
- enhance opportunities for both assigned and casual reading
- provide choice in self-selecting reading materials for self-engagement
- strengthen and encourage authentic literate exchanges among students
- provide access to digitized reading materials that foster the development of technological literacy skills
- facilitate opportunities to validate and promote the acceptance and inclusion of diverse students' identities and experiences
- create opportunities to cultivate an informed citizenry

Building a Classroom Library

So many books! So little time! A library rich in book topics, genres, and levels allows all readers access to material they want to read and can read. According to Routman (2003), "An adequate classroom library will have at least two hundred books, but an excellent library will have more than a thousand" (67). It is hard to become a book expert without spending hours in a library, scrolling on social media (check out hashtags such as #IMWAYR and #nf10for10), reading blogs and professional books, and attending conferences and local chapter meetings for your state literacy association. Today, children's literature is more dynamic than ever, and offers its readers many avenues for pleasure, reflection, adventure, and emotional engagement. Taking time to become acquainted with newer books will

help you create a library that can meet the needs of your readers and build excitement for reading.

Random book lists aren't very helpful unless they are fully annotated, providing information about genre, theme, plot summaries, awards, areas of interest, and reading levels. Quality literature today is often timely and relevant, and every day we're seeing more and more books that are inclusive, diverse, and socially conscious. Websites with book titles that represent a wide range of cultures and experiences, such as We Need Diverse Books (diversebooks.org), Colorín Colorado (colorincolorado.org), and Jane Addams Peace Association (https://www. janeaddamschildrensbookaward.org), can get you started, but you will still need to do the work of actually reading the books you're considering for your classroom library collection. Be sure to look at NCTE's *Language Arts* journal (NCTE.org) to browse the Children's Literature Reviews in each monthly issue where titles are explored in detail around themes/topics such as "Orbis Pictus Awards for Outstanding Nonfiction" and "Children's Literature to Support Critical Literacies Engagement."

TEACHER TIP: Ask your librarian for suggestions of books you can "book talk" for each new area or genre you're studying. Ask if they would post book recommendations on index cards around the library in appropriate locations or highlight some on a bulletin board that is eye level for students. Invite local librarians to visit your school or class to introduce the public library as a resource for books and share information about summer reading programs.

Probably the best way to begin this journey is to make friends with your school and local librarians. They can be so helpful! You might ask them to help you create a stack of recently published books. You could ask them to share a stack of fiction books and, the next month, a stack of nonfiction books. Requesting book stacks by the same author is a wonderful way to begin an author study investigation. A genre stack is also a great idea, especially if you poll your students to find out what they are reading or not reading and see a need to broaden their reading tastes. Ask for a new stack each month—that's doable! Picture books are written for a large audience, and while some target K–1 readers, many are appropriate for readers in grades 2–8. There are also wonderful biographies written as picture books to help students get interested in that genre—including books like *Feed Your Mind: A Story of August Wilson* by Jennifer Bryant, *One Wish: Fatima al-Fihri and the World's Oldest University* by M. O. Yuksel, *Whoosh! Lonnie Johnson's Super-Soaking Stream of Inventions* by Chris Barton, *Dream Builder: The Story of Architect Philip Freelon* by Kelly Starling Lyons, and *Ida B. Wells, Voice of Truth: Educator, Feminist, and Anti-Lynching Civil Rights Leader* by Michelle Duster.

Finally, get recommendations from people in the know. Often, a trusted peer, literacy coaches, or classroom teachers who know your goals can offer great book suggestions. For more support in building a classroom library, see **Appendix E: Classroom Library Thinking/Talking Points**; and if you are starting from scratch, don't know where to begin, or are weeding books from a library collection you've inherited, here are some additional hints to guide you:

1. Look for books that are visually interesting and have colorful photos or illustrations.
2. Pull a few books that will make great read-alouds and place them on a separate shelf to save for experiencing as a whole group (you can eventually have a second and third copy of your favorite read-aloud selections your students want to read independently).
3. For K–2 classroom libraries, include books with effective repetition, a pattern, and sometimes rhyme.
4. Look for books with strong characters that children can relate to and be inspired by.
5. Books with a roller coaster of emotions that engage young readers are keepers!
6. Look for humor! Look for action!

7. Award-winning books recognized by the American Library Association and other awards lists, such as Coretta Scott King, Orbis-Pictus, Pura Belpré, and the Newbery medal are good choices.

8. Books in a series (e.g., a trilogy) sustain interest over time and create readers.

9. Books that represent diverse cultures in contemporary settings— where your students can see themselves in the pages of a book— are essential!

10. Check the copyright dates and consider if your collection is dated and needs new life.

Building Inclusive Classroom Libraries

While we want to have books in our library that reflect the students in our class, we also want to give children opportunities to meet people unlike themselves (Fleming, 2019) in the books they read, opening a world of new possibilities and understandings. To this end, we suggest constantly reflecting on the books you showcase, asking yourself, "Is diversity a feature of my library throughout the year and not just during observance periods like Black History Month, Women's History Month, Earth Day, and Martin Luther King Day?" When concerns are raised about specific texts, give them a critical eye, do your homework on their origins, and seek clarification from experts whose lived experiences speak from a place of authority. If books support misconceptions or out-of-date information, weed and replace them with books that can do a better job of representing our students and the real facts. With the wonderfully diverse populations inherent in our school systems, making texts relevant to students is critical. Books can provide a sense of belonging for all students. They develop awareness, empathy, and compassion for others. They allow students to celebrate cultures and experiences that are like or different from their own. They can even inspire our students to write their own stories! As you consider this importance of inclusivity, think about where your classroom library is strong and where you may need to fill in some gaps.

Video 6.2 ▶

Broadening Our Definition of Diversity

Poet **Janet Wong** relates a childhood story to help us rethink how children identify themselves and connect with books.

Video 6.3 ▶

Vetting Books for Classroom Library

Assistant Superintendent **Dr. Mwynyewe Dawan** talks about the big responsibility educators have when deciding to choose books for a classroom library.

TEACHER TIP: The classroom library is not static. Books should be regularly rotated in and out of the library. When you decide to do some "weeding" in your library, ask a colleague to help you. Discuss the reasons to keep or remove a book or series from your stacks. Some books are worth keeping, while others, even though they were celebrated at one time, may need to go and be replaced with something newer and more diverse.

Organizing Your Classroom Library

The organization of your library collection is an important step to consider. Well-organized libraries with clear groupings and engaging labels ensure that readers can find favorites and discover new titles. There are many organizational systems you might use, but eventually you will need to choose what works best for you and your reading community. Will you sort by topic? Genre? Author? Theme? Alphabetically by title? You could spend entire days sorting books and creating bin labels all on your own before your students arrive, or . . . you could give your students ownership of their library by inviting them to organize the books and create the classroom library. In this way, the reading community is tasked with grouping books in ways that make sense for them, placing books into containers, labeling the containers, and then deciding how and where to display books on shelves. While this is a messy, often loud endeavor, there are definite benefits that make it worth the effort. As children sort and unpack boxes they begin to discover books they have previously read and enthusiastically endorse them to peers. They uncover titles they have been waiting to read and soon begin to build a stack of new titles and genres they want to read.

Figure 6.4 Third graders spend quality time organizing their classroom library, making recommendations for additions and deletions.

This activity not only introduces the children to books but is also great for community-building. As the class works, nudge them to read the book blurbs to discover genres and topics and encourage them to come up with sorting possibilities that make sense to them as they plan out where their books should be placed and why.

Figure 6.5 Students sort books into categories and series, placing them into bins for the library. Writing out book descriptions on the bin label helps children make book choices.

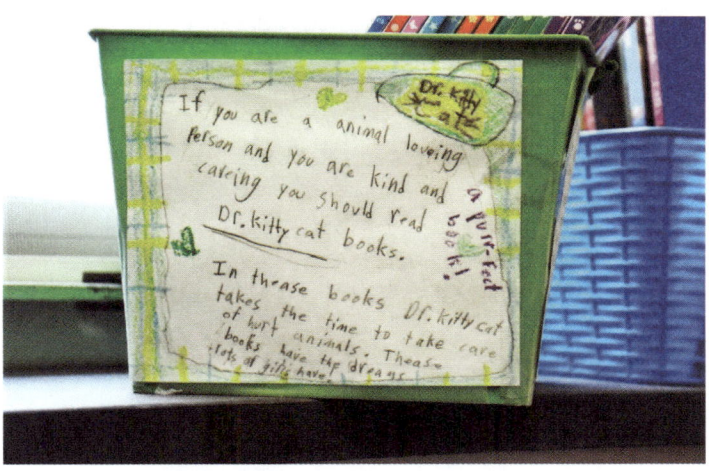

Of course, not all teachers are comfortable with this process. Without proper planning it can certainly become chaotic and time-consuming. Still, consider your level of comfort. Is this something you'd like to try? If you're not 100% on board yet, could you let students sort through just some of the books and decide how to group them in the library? Maybe you have already sorted the books into bins; why not let students create the labels after studying the books in the bins? Or, consider letting students place books and bins in strategic locations around the room to encourage book choice. Finding a way to include your students in this process gives them ownership of the library and can go a long way toward building excitement for and engagement in reading.

Figure 6.6 Possibilities for organizing your classroom library might include a reading nook enclosed by bins of books on shelves, or a wall of book bins for a tiny classroom (teacher rotates bins so the ones on a higher shelf are eventually on a lower shelf), or a special area where books are sorted into bins by author.

Should Classroom Libraries Be Leveled?

We understand that in kindergarten through second grade, classroom libraries may need to have sections that are leveled. Leveled texts can help children choose books that present limited challenges so they can work on reading goals and help them select texts they are more likely to be able to read and comprehend (Seravallo, 2018). We want children to practice skills, and to enjoy reading; but at the same time, our children need to know they are readers—not a level. You might ask, "Do I need to assign a level to every book in my classroom library?" and "Can students choose books that are sometimes too easy and sometimes difficult for them?" Miller and Sharp (2018) suggest that relying too heavily on leveling systems may "deny *readers* valuable opportunities to fine-tune their book selection under our guidance" (51). The word *guidance* is important! Teaching children how to self-select books for independent reading, and offering support with book selection, is a role we play as teachers. Knowing our students as readers and knowing the books in our libraries allows us to guide children to make informed book choices. Routman (2018) suggests, "Leveled texts can be useful for guided reading and for students still struggling to choose books they can read, but for most of us, having a wide range of choices works best" (50–51). For example, Ethan loves to draw comics but struggles to sustain reading for longer periods of time, so you might guide him to graphic novels that are easier before introducing him to *El Deafo* by CeCe Bell. Sometimes, students possess the background knowledge to select a nonfiction book on a high-interest topic. While these students may not always be able to read the running text, they can read the text features—such as photos, diagrams, maps, charts, and drawings with labels—and make meaning from this more complex text. In *Beyond Leveled Texts*, the authors tell us, "It is important for students to understand that there are many reasons a book is right for them at the time. It's not about levels. Often, there are more complex reasons to consider. If we can help students be in tune with their lives as readers, they will also be able to figure out when a book is not just right for them and why" (Szymusiak, Sibberson, and Koch, 2008).

> **TEACHER TIP:** Display the "just right" books, or books most of your class can read independently, at eye level and remember to move books in and out of your classroom library as your readers grow throughout the year.

Creating the Excitement for Reading

Have you ever shared a book as a read-aloud and then noticed how some students begin to bring in their own copies, found in school and public libraries or bookstores? There is nothing better than favorite read-alouds being reread by students during independent reading time. Other ways of recommending favorites, such as student reviews, book talks, loved trilogies, or sharing books from longer series, can create this same level of excitement for reading. Though this experience often happens spontaneously, there are plenty of ways we can create classroom libraries that ignite a similar buzz for reading.

> **TEACHER TIP:** When reading aloud, try some classics as well as newer titles. Libraries usually have multiple copies of these books in their libraries and children will be able to access them easily. Reading aloud the first book in a series is another way to hook kids. But be sure to have multiple copies of the next book in your library for your readers. Book two is sure to be a hot title!

Sometimes, this begins with enticing readers visually. Take a cue from your local library when organizing books. At Brenda's local library there is a wall of new books prominently displayed. The display shows the book covers and organizes them by fiction genres and nonfiction selections.

Consider placing your new titles under a sign in your classroom, not necessarily in your library, that indicates these are new titles. Then watch the excitement as your students recognize titles and authors or topics they are interested in reading.

Helping children discover books and authors is one of the great joys of a reading workshop. Children gravitate to visual displays created to introduce books and authors. Labeling books with "seals of approval" or "awards" given by classmates creates a buzz for books in classrooms and helps children when selecting books. In Brenda's room, children have been known to leave a notecard in the book naming the book a personal recommendation (e.g., "Melanie's pick"). Students also create "book reviews" as labels for book bins. These reviews and ratings allow others to make a more informed choice, since they not only show the book title or series but give a short summary or endorsement and entice the reader to select the book.

You might also consider organizing shelves with displays like the virtual shelves on Amazon—*If you liked . . . you might want to try . . . .* Children who like reading a particular series or genre often want more once they are hooked. Creating a shelf that displays one book that children gravitate to and then adding similar books they might want to try helps them choose books and builds reading excitement. Giving children the opportunity to curate these shelves leads to ownership in addition to the already budding excitement.

This last note brings up an important final point about harnessing excitement in your reading community. Instead of being the only person who makes classroom library choices, invite your students to help you do this. Some of them are nonfiction experts—they know the sports books, the animal books, the bizarre-but-true topics that are quite fascinating to their peers. Some of them know series books and others know more than you can imagine about fantasy. The range of their interests can only help you diversify your collection in ways that appeal to all the readers in your classroom.

What Is Reading Workshop?

Two words come to mind when I think of reading workshop—community and joy. As a first grade teacher thirty years ago, I knew little about how to teach reading in a workshop, but the words of Donald Graves, the father of the writing workshop, guided my instruction. I knew that children needed choice in the books they read, time to read, and a response (feedback) from the teacher. So every reading workshop began with a minilesson, followed by children reading independently. As children read, I would circulate around the room conferring with children about their reading and their thinking. We were a community of readers where everyone could participate with a book they chose and wanted to read, and consequently our classroom was a place of joy. Children loved to read, they saw themselves as competent readers, and they read a lot.

Gail Ryan,
Retired Principal and Literacy Consultant

Book Shopping

In order for the independent reading portion of the reading workshop to run smoothly, readers will need a thriving classroom library and routines for purposely selecting books for themselves. To this end, setting aside intentional time for book shopping is important. When can you schedule book shopping in your classroom? Readers could book-shop first thing in the morning as part of their morning routine or during snack-break time. The end of the school day, while students wait for buses to arrive, has also proven to be a time to linger in the classroom library and choose books.

Notice when children shop—and how and why! Are they shopping to avoid reading? Are they shopping daily? Are they just wandering your library? Are they grabbing a book quickly and engaging in "fake reading"? This could signal that their choices are not appropriate for them or that they have not yet developed stamina and endurance for reading books of certain genres or lengths. It could also tell you that your library lacks engaging options for some of your readers.

> **TEACHER TIP:** Our primary grade readers need multiple books in their book boxes or baggies—books that they can read and reread, books that may require some work, and books they are browsing. This means book shopping happens more often. Setting up a schedule to book-shop—when and how—is an important management tool. Create a schedule, but be flexible. Keeping kids reading is the goal.

A suggestion box may help you add books to your classroom library that will make book shopping a successful, fun process for all your readers and, at the same time, promote student ownership, making them part of the process of creating a classroom library for every student. Do you need some books about nonfiction topics like extreme sports and fossil hunters? Many students prefer nonfiction, even kindergarten and first grade students. To that end, you might want to begin a section in your library for great nonfiction magazines such as *Zoobooks*; *National Geographic*; *EcoKids Planet*; *Ranger Rick*; *Kids Discover*; *Astronomy for Kids* (a new magazine also available as a digital download); and *Kids, Code, and Computer Science*. Re-examining your students' reading interest surveys will also help you consider new books or magazines to include in your school library collection.

As you continue to refine your classroom library, think about how variety and comfort can entice readers to book-shop. Does your library contain books written in verse or as a graphic novel? Does your library reflect the population and interests of your class? Do you have more than just the first book of a series? Students find their confidence by reading books in a series as they become familiar with the characters, writing style, settings, and story lines. They know how the story goes and can count on characters behaving in certain ways. With each subsequent book, the series reader can not only predict more easily how the story will go or how a character may act, but they also become aware of character changes and growth across the series. These readers eventually become experts and guides for their classmates who want to read a particular series. Reading series books often helps striving readers acquire the higher-end literacy skills needed to read more complex texts. Consider choosing the first book in a series as a read-aloud every now and then or organizing book clubs around a series to promote them. The starter list of favorite series books in **Figure 6.7** is a great place to begin.

Figure 6.7

Series Books Readers Love

Primary: (Grades K-3)

Mercy Watson by Kate DiCamillo

Jada Jones by Kelly Starling Lyons

Elephant and Piggy by Mo Willems

Inspector Flytrap by Tom Angleberger

Lulu by Hilary McKay

Katie Woo by Fran Manushkin

Keena Ford by Melissa Thompson

Elray Jakes by Sally Warner

Kingdom of Wrenly by Jordan Quinn

Miami Jackson series by Patricia and Frederick McKissack

Freddy Ramos Takes Off, book #1 in the Zapato Power series by Jaqueline Jules

Intermediate: (Grades 3–6)

Keeper of the Lost Cities by Shannon Messenger

Penderwicks by Jeanne Birdsall

Land of Stories by Chris Colfer

George Handel, in the Getting to Know the World's Greatest Composers series by Mike Venezia–see also his Getting to Know the World's Greatest Artists and Getting to Know the U.S. Presidents series

The Maze of Bones, book #1 in The 39 Clues series by Rick Riordan

I Survived series by Lauren Tarshis

Who Was. . . ? series by various authors/Penguin Books (nonfiction)

Who Would Win? series by Jerry Pallotta

Smile (graphic novel) by Raina Telgemeier

Jasmine Toguchi, Mochi Queen, book #1 in the Jasmine Toguchi series by Debbi Michiko Florence

Helping Children Make Strong Book Choices

There's no mistake about it—reading inspires, entertains, and educates us. But how do we choose the right book to read? When we teach students how to choose their independent reads, we support them in finding books that have personal relevance while honoring their individual reading identities. According to the International Literacy Association (ILA; 2018), "Ninety-one percent of children ages 6–17 report that 'my favorite books are the ones that I have picked out myself'" (6). We know that our striving and reluctant readers need this choice and ownership in order to feel that they are readers. When they discover a book in their school or classroom library collection that is personally relevant to their experiences and interests, they get a clear message that they matter and that books help them celebrate these interests and experiences. When readers have the freedom to choose their own books, they are motivated to work through the challenges these texts might present. How can we best teach our students how to self-select an independent read?

When children struggle with book choice, we refer to interest surveys (see **Appendices B** and **C** for interest surveys) completed in the beginning of the year. These help us tap into student likes and dislikes, guiding our suggestions. It is also helpful to consider reading ability when offering suggestions. Offering a variety of choices gives students more ownership and buy-in. Consider laying out a few book choices, and then teach children to read the book blurb on the back of the book. Readers will most definitely be influenced by their peers, so getting a friend to add to the recommendation will go a long way. Another helpful way to find a good book is to look for books that appeal specifically by genre or author. If you are a mystery reader, you'll like books that are fast-paced and thrilling. If you prefer fantasies, you'll be ready for oodles of rich description, a focus on character development, and moving at a slower pace. Students will often find books in a series appealing because they know the author's style, know the characters, and understand how the plot is constructed.

Video 6.4 ▶

Picture Books for Everyone

Sixth grade teacher and children's book author **Frank Murphy** discusses the value of placing picture books in upper grade classroom libraries.

Picture books by authors such as Floyd Cooper, Patricia Polacco, Jacqueline Woodson, Kelly Starling Lyons, and Allen Say can be good choices for upper elementary school students who struggle with reading, because the length of the book is not daunting but the interest level is appropriate.

In reading workshop, it is important to teach our readers not only how to navigate the library but how to choose books they want to read and are able to read. We know children choose books with different purposes in mind. Teaching children how to make these choices gives them an important life-long skill. In **Appendix D: Minilesson Template and Samples**, we include a sample minilesson on choosing books you might replicate to get this conversation started.

Choosing to Abandon a Book

Choice belongs to the reader. We can offer suggestions, provide guidance, and even physically hand the books we love to our readers, but if the book isn't a match for the reader, it won't be read or enjoyed. Choice in reading workshop means students also have the right to abandon a book. Providing guidelines for abandoning a book helps readers own their choices. In a conference, invite students to talk about their choice to abandon a particular book and hear from them about their decision.

Figure 6.8

When Would I Abandon a Book?

- I don't know enough about the topic or setting to understand the ideas.
- I've lost interest (I may return to it in the future).
- I've changed my mind because it is too hard—I don't know a lot of the words.
- The book is too easy—I need more of a challenge.
- The book is too long—I've been reading it all week, and I haven't gotten hooked!
- I don't think the main character(s) is believable (or I simply don't like them).
- I cannot connect with or identify with any of the characters in the story.
- I need a more current book to read about _____ (for example, space travel).

- I thought it was going to be about one thing, but it turned out to be about something else.
- I am super-excited to read something else! (A new book, for instance, in the school or classroom library or a book that is being passed around and it's your turn to read it.)

TEACHER TIP: Watch for students who are abandoning books too often—this could be a red flag indicating that these students are not making effective first choices and may need your help in finding their next book.

Book Talks to Showcase Books in a Classroom Library

A great way to introduce children to books is through book talks. They are a powerful way to build and sustain your community of readers. According to Miller and Sharp (2018), "The only thing readers enjoy almost as much as reading is talking about the books with other readers" (109). Research shows that peer recommendations are the most powerful way we can get kids to read on their own (Williams and McDaniel 2017).

Beginning with book talks as soon as possible will help you create a community of readers eager to begin their reading journey with you while, at the same time, showcasing all the wonderful titles in your classroom library collection. Think about your own readerly life. It's probably driven by suggestions from personal friends and family members, people you follow on social media, or blogs such as *Nerdy Book Club*, and colleagues you trust as readers. This is the case in our classrooms as well. Students often want to read what their friends are reading. Regularly scheduled book talks (we prefer once a month, but you'll find what works best for your group) can motivate our most striving readers to try a book and, in general, increase the volume of books borrowed from your classroom library.

Remember to keep the expectations for book talks simple:

- Finish reading the entire book before book before talking it.
- Don't give away too much information—especially the ending!
- Keep it short, interesting, and suspenseful.

Some modeling helps here. We usually return to a read-aloud we have used in the first week of school so the students are familiar with the content and can understand what is highlighted or what emotions the book might elicit (humorous, sad, happy, etc.). Here, through discussion and modeling, students can learn the importance of not sharing the ending in a storybook.

FORMATS HELP CHILDREN PREPARE FOR A BOOK TALK

In addition to a few simple expectations, questions and statements to ponder provide some general guidance and structure for book talks. These three categories—fiction, informational, and first-account book talks—present some basic possibilities, but many scaffolds can be used as a starting point.

Fiction Book

- Use a question to hook your audience, like, "Have you ever been in a really spooky library?"
- Describe the setting, and one of the main characters.
- Introduce the problem or conflict.
- Talk about an incident in the book.
- Be sure to give the complete title and author. Target audience: Who would like this book? Why?
- Build interest, but don't give away the ending.

Informational Book

- Use a question to hook your audience, like, "Have you ever seen a spider the size of a dinner plate?"
- Share a few interesting tidbits using the question markers to help you: who, where, when, what, how, why.
- Be sure to give the complete title and author.
- Know your audience: Who would like this book? Why?

The First-Person Account

- Become one of the characters in the book or the person in the biography or autobiography and talk about what happens to you.
- Start with a question or strong statement to hook your audience, like, "What would you do if a friend challenged you to eat worms every day for fifteen days in order to win a bet?"
- Talk about the problem or conflict from your character's point of view.
- Describe an incident.
- Be sure to give the complete title and author.
- Target audience: Who would like this book? Why?

Modeling a book talk for your students creates a community where everyone is a reader and contributor. Choose a book you think the kids in your class will enjoy, maybe something that is new to your library or a series you think they will enjoy. (You might present a few book-talk titles that you're considering for your next read-aloud and then let the kids choose which book you will read.) Write notes for your book talk using one of the scaffolds mentioned earlier. Then model by giving the talk to your students. To help you get started, we include sample book talks for *The Undefeated* and *How to Eat Fried Worms* below, along with video links to a few others.

 **Book Talk:** *The Undefeated*

As you look at the title and cover of this book (*show book cover*) your brain swims with questions and wonderings—Who are the people? What did they defeat? This book will take you on an historical journey and introduce you to African Americans who are unforgettable, undeniable, unflappable, unafraid, and more. Follow the poem through time to learn about men and women who sacrificed much, encountered hardships, yet never gave up. Instead, they rose up to make a difference. *The Undefeated* by Kwame Alexander is ready to introduce you to individuals who endure, strive, and thrive.

 **Book Talk:** *How to Eat Fried Worms*

So, do you like them fried, boiled, breaded, or just plain raw? "What?" you ask. WORMS! If you are like Billy, you may just learn to eat them any old way. For a bet of $50 to buy a mini-bike . . . would you eat them? Find out if Billy wins the bet of eating fifteen worms in fifteen days despite all the sneaky tactics Joe and Allen use to make Billy wonder if he can do it. A great book to read anywhere you go—short chapters make it possible to read in the car, at the dentist's office, or before you get ready for bed. Don't miss *How to Eat Fried Worms* by Thomas Rockwell . . . unless, of course, you have a weak stomach!

Video 6.5 ▶

Book Talk Example Book Talk:

Sophia shares an excerpt as part of her book talk.

Video 6.6 ▶

Book Talk Example Book Talk:

Makynli stirs interest by engaging her peers with a book talk about a beloved graphic novel.

Video 6.7 ▶

Book Talk Example — *Book Talk:*

Kameron shares a book talk to introduce peers to *Hilo Book 1: The Boy Who Crashed to Earth.*

Video 6.8 ▶

Book Talk Example — *Book Talk:*

In his book talk, Nicholas sets a high-impact scene, then leads his listeners on with questions meant to pique their interest.

Book talk models and trailers can also be found online. Using sites like Bookopolis, Biblionasium, and Scholastic, children can view book talks and get book recommendations. YouTube is a great resource for finding more information on how to create book talks and view book talks and trailers that will inspire readers. For instance, you can search for Olivia Van Ledtje, a young changemaker who inspires kids and educators to make use of digital tools to share their favorite books and connect with others in faraway places. Share her book talks with your students through her *Livbits* Vimeo Channel. You might also consider subscribing to Colby Sharp's YouTube channel where Colby gives book talks of his favorite books and those of his students. These book talks provide great models for our students and will give you some new titles for your classroom library and read-aloud selections.

Once they're ready, invite children to prepare and give a book talk for their peers. Taking the time to help students prepare and practice will help ensure book talks create a buzz for books. For younger students, try placing them in partnerships or small groups to share a favorite book. Book talks are easier for these early readers if they have the book to look at and show to their classmates. Students can talk about why they liked the book and who they think might like to read it. Talking about target audiences is usually easy for these readers. Would dog lovers read this book? Who enjoys team sports? Are there classmates who love a particular author?

Children, like adults, want to read what their peers are reading. By offering time to share formally and informally with classmates, choice becomes a social dimension in the reading community. After Jack book-talked the first book in the book series Origami Yoda by Tom Angleberger, the books flew out of the book bin Jack had created for the series in Brenda's classroom library. Soon the school library was bereft of the books as well, so Julius convinced his mother to stop at the local library so "everyone who wants to read the books can." Sharing the joy of books and reading is contagious!

Final Thoughts

If we want engaged readers who are filled with wonder and curiosity, we need to make our classroom library the star of the show. In this chapter, we've given you lots of ideas for encouraging your classroom readership through thoughtfully designed and curated libraries and opportunities for readers to book-shop and share their favorite titles through book talks. With a well-organized classroom library and a current collection that's representative of all the children who sit in your classrooms, you can ensure that your independent reading time (see **Chapter 7**) is best utilized by all your students. The classroom library is essential to all the effective teaching and learning that takes place in your reading workshop and across your learning day.

Stop and Reflect

1. How does your library reflect the students in your class and encourage readers to browse and find books? Do you need to make some physical changes to give students ownership of the space and increase usership?

2. What would it be like to schedule time for book talks in your classroom? What type of modeling and supports would you need to have in place so your students could be successful? How often should book talks occur? When would students practice their book talks? How can book talks be shared with families, other classrooms, or the entire school community?

Something to Try

Invite a colleague to do individual audits of your libraries, using the Classroom Library Thinking/Talking Points (see **Appendix E**). After each of you has completed the survey alone, share and discuss your results. What do you notice? Are there some gaps that need to be filled? Can you take some steps together to enhance or spruce up your library? Support each other as you move forward.

Chapter 7

Independent Reading Time: Supporting Readers at Work

Our students will only become fluent, comprehending readers who develop deep engagement, stamina, competence, content knowledge, and self-monitoring abilities if and when we prioritize free-choice, independent reading every day.

> **– Regie Routman,**
> *Literacy Essentials: Engagement, Excellence, and Equity for All Learners*

"Norah, what are you reading and what page are you on?"

"I'm reading *The Sisters Grimm* number 2, and I'm almost done, so can I go get the next one?" Her teacher nods, affirming her request, and moves to the next student, Joel, who tells Mrs. Jay he is reading the *Fly Guy* series and holds up three books, waving them excitedly. Mrs. Jay notices he doesn't have a page in a specific book to report but seems to be just flipping between books, so she makes a note to herself to check in with Joel as soon as she finishes taking the status of the class. After a quick check in, she scans the room. Children are scattered around the classroom space; on bean bag chairs, lying on the floor, sitting at tables, or propped up on pillows. Each has settled in for their independent reading time. They have their current book choice as well as one or two that are "on deck" in their book baggies. Sticky notes and

Video 7.1 ▶

Rationale for Independent Reading

Past principal and literacy specialist **Gail Ryan** shares her enthusiasm and beliefs about independent reading time.

Video 7.2 ▶

Value of Independent Reading Time

Assistant Superintendent **Dr. Mwynyewe Dawan** highlights the importance of independent reading to develop lifelong readers.

reader's notebooks are at the ready. With clipboard in hand, Mrs. Jay cruises the room, making brief stops to check in with students before moving on to her first small group meeting and conferences. The class is settled, eyes on texts. There is a feeling of important work being done as well as a sense of enjoyment.

Why It's Important to Give Students Time to Read Independently

Independent reading time is a time for students to read a book they have chosen, a time to practice skills and strategies that have been taught, a time to talk about books and reading with their teacher . . . a time to be immersed in the joy of reading. Researcher-authors Pam Allyn and Ernest Morrell (2016) tell us, "Reading is a great equalizer that has the power to break down the typical barriers to education, those invisible walls built around coveted zip codes and elite institutions." If we want *all* our students to be to be immersed in the actual act of reading daily, we need to set aside intentional time for this in our reading block. This routine helps students develop positive attitudes about reading through a wide range of interesting choices and positive experiences that increase motivation and engagement for reading.

Many reading experts would agree with Richard Allington (2002) when he notes that "extensive reading is critical to the development of reading proficiency" (742). But how much time is enough to make a difference? According to the International Literacy Association (ILA; 2018), "independent reading must occur each day for at least 15 minutes. Without this frequency and duration, students may not develop appropriate stamina. As little as 15 minutes of in-school reading has a profound impact; students who read independently for that amount of time significantly increased their reading performance, with more profound gains for below-average readers" (6).

Figure 7.1 This first grader is enjoying his independent reading time. Today was his turn for the rocking chair, a coveted spot for reading.

Daily independent reading time provides the opportunity for students to experiment with and develop the skills and strategies that teachers demonstrate during the minilesson. We suggest pushing beyond ILA's recommended fifteen minutes to twenty minutes (or more!) of independent reading daily, especially for upper elementary grades. You can always start with a smaller amount of time or adjust according to grade level needs and what might be sustainable for your students. If you begin with ten minutes and everyone is still reading at the end of that time, try giving the class an additional five minutes. This block of time allows students to enter what Nancy Atwell (2007) calls "the reading zone"—that space in time when students get "lost in a book" and are not aware of the passing of time. It is during daily independent reading time that students build stamina and endurance for reading. This is particularly important for our striving readers.

Of course, opportunities to read across the day include guided reading lessons, science, and social studies time and more. Though many teachers assign some amount of independent reading as homework each night, we've found that our less motivated readers do not rush home from school to curl up with a good book. In fact, we cannot be sure they are actually doing any reading at home. But, if we build in time to read independently at school, we can help students find a good book (if they need that help) and observe readerly behaviors to help them become more skilled at being proficient readers. An established, regular independent reading block makes time for students to practice the strategies and skills they've learned in minilessons, both consciously and subconsciously, and for teachers to differentiate instruction through roving conferences and small group interactions. In *Good Choice! Supporting Independent Reading and Response K–6*, author/educator Tony Stead (2008) reminds us that when we create "a time for independent reading from the onset of the school year, children not only build up stamina for reading, but also see it as an important and pleasurable component of their daily lives" (5). In essence, our students learn to read by reading. With access to a wonderful classroom and school library (see **Chapter 6**) and daily time to read books they select, students will grow as readers and develop lifelong reading habits.

Figure 7.2 When finding a spot to read independently, some children choose to read at their desks, depending on the purpose of their reading. As they grow, they become more adept at determining the appropriate location for their independent reading.

Figure 7.3 Creating a distinct space for readers to curl up and get comfortable with a book invites them to get lost in the experience of reading.

TEACHER TIP: Intrinsically motivated readers read because it gives them enjoyment or satisfaction in some way. We need to find ways to motivate our students to read other than contests, prizes, and pizza parties. Giving children our full attention as they respond is all they need to feel affirmed and motivated to read.

What Are Students Doing During Independent Reading?

Independent reading is sacred time in the reading workshop, and setting expectations is important. Taking the time in the beginning of the year to help children understand the work they will do during this time, and how, will help you accomplish your goals for reading workshop and increase student independence. You might consider bringing the class together to create an anchor chart that lists what the independent reading *looks like, sounds like, and feels like.* For children who have had workshop experiences, this exercise reminds them of reading habits that have been used successfully in previous classrooms. Children who are newer to a workshop format will need more time and teacher modeling to learn habits that increase reading stamina and reading focus. One strategy you might start out with is to send students off to read independently for fifteen minutes and then regroup on the floor to create an anchor chart listing actions that helped them be successful during independent reading time as well as distractions that hindered their success. Post the chart as a reminder of what the class, as a reading community, has determined are the expectations for independent reading time. In this way, your students become the standard setters and have ownership of this time.

BUILDING STAMINA

Helping children read independently for extended periods of time is one goal for the workshop. Jennifer Serravallo reminds us in her book *The Reading Strategies Book: Your Everything Guide to Developing Skilled Readers* (2015, 44) that "engagement is everything." If children are not reading during independent reading time, they will not make the progress we are hoping for and working toward. Helping children increase their stamina—the amount of time they can sustain their reading—becomes part of the work done in independent reading time. Children need realistic time expectations and strategies to help them increase their reading stamina. Supporting this provides instructional opportunities for procedural minilessons, small group conversations, or individual conference focus points.

Strategies to build stamina can range from finding a smart place to read so you can concentrate to figuring out your next steps to make the best use of this time. One strategy you might try is to create a class graph that shows the number of minutes the class reads during independent reading time. Children will see the bars grow over time and feel their success as a community of readers. Older children can keep their own graphs. Reading the graph and drawing conclusions from the data is important and could be used to set class goals as well as individual goals. Brenda has also asked children to record the number of minutes they read at home.

As you consider building stamina, recognize that not all of your readers can sit for extended periods of time—kids need to move!

Be sure to set reasonable and realistic goals for the group of children you're teaching. And remember, there will always be a reader or two who needs more specific support with building stamina. For example, in a conference, Brenda and her student, Mickey, were able to establish a time frame for taking a break while reading independently. Giving him a set amount of time to read, and establishing a signal system for movement, helped Brenda maintain her conferring schedule and kept Mickey reading. In the beginning his goal was ten minutes of reading with a quick standing stretch. As the year progressed, they reevaluated this goal together periodically, increasing the amount of time he could read before a movement break each time.

Other children in the class, like Kathleen, struggled with stamina because her mind wandered. Helping children recognize when they start to lose their reading focus, and giving them strategies to re-enter the text, helps to increase their stamina as well as focus. Kathleen would place sticky notes in the text to indicate spots to stop reading and retell what she'd read so far to herself. With this tool, Kathleen was able to self-monitor and soon learned that her book choice often hindered her ability to stay focused on the text. Examining a child's reading habits; location, time, and book choice can help you work with them to create goals that will increase stamina and bring greater joy to independent reading time.

> **What Is Reading Workshop?**
>
> For me, reading workshop is a time for students to practice the skills and strategies of reading in a way that makes reading work for them. It is entirely different than the way I (and many others, I'm sure) learned to read. It is not based on identical texts followed by comprehension questions, but about an authentic reading experience. Students pick their own books based on interests, abilities, goals, and personalities; just as adult readers so often do. The workshop time is used to support and stretch readers with minilessons, read-alouds, conferences, strategy groups, and book talks, all of which can be applied directly to students' independent reading. It is a time to strengthen both the skills of reading, and the enjoyment of it.
>
> **Marissa Moyer,**
> Grade 3 teacher, Franconia Elementary

WRITING IN RESPONSE TO READING

Though students largely work on reading during independent reading time, they'll also need opportunities to write in response to their reading or complete book club work during this time. Readers will need to be taught when it is appropriate to write, what they might be writing about (see **Figure 7.5**), and how to get back quickly to reading. It's important to teach children to use their notebooks as a way to jot about their thinking while reading (see **Chapter 5**). Students will use their reading response journals to record thoughts as well as respond to their reading in a variety of ways. Since different children have different abilities and goals, their notebooks will be used differently. Some may use their notebook to place sticky notes of important plot points in their fictional book and then use them during conferences to retell and discuss the text. Others will prefer to maintain their focus, stopping and jotting periodically as they read. And, some may need your guidance, so they don't spend all their reading time writing. Teaching children when it is appropriate to stop and jot is something you will want to think about. A common practice you might consider is to establish a specific time during your workshop for writing in response to reading, setting a timer to signify when it's time for the group to return to reading. Experiment with different time slots to see what works for you and your students—in the middle of the reading time, near the conclusion of reading time, or as a concluding segment of the reading workshop.

Figure 7.4 Students use part of their independent reading time to make entries in their reader's notebooks in response to the texts they are reading.

Figure 7.5

Different Ways Students Can Respond to Reading

1 Drawings with labels and/or speech bubbles to capture a favorite scene
2 Plot summary
3 Scene from a text for Reader's Theater
4 Illustration study to discuss how an illustration layers meaning and adds to the text
5 Photo essay/picture essay (use with nonfiction) to explore a topic and what you learned without using words
6 Multimedia presentation as a book trailer to advertise or recommend the book
7 News or feature article (used with nonfiction) as a summary tool or to highlight new learning
8 Book talk/book review
9 Biographical sketch of a main character or favorite character
10 Found poem to respond to a character's actions or summarize

If readers are having difficulty getting started writing during independent reading, it might be a good idea to provide questions to get them thinking. Using a basic set of prompts for several months will help students improve in the way they respond. For instance, the following prompts might help students to begin to write about the fiction book they are reading and use their written responses to encourage them to actively participate in whole or small group discussions:

- Did the story/nonfiction text end the way you expected it to end? What clues did the author give to you?
- This story/nonfiction text reminds me of . . . because . . . .
- What is the author trying to tell us by writing this story/nonfiction text? What are the life lessons?
- One thing I learned from the story/nonfiction text that surprised me was . . . . It surprised because . . . .
- I used to think . . . but after reading the story/nonfiction I now think . . . .

You may decide to collect students' writing every few weeks and skim and scan to get a feel for how they are handling this way of responding. Remember, students should not be expected to write during every independent reading block or even after completing each book. As adult readers, we don't always end our reading time by writing a thought or summary of what we read.

> **TEACHER TIP:** To make written responses more appealing to students, keep a supply of colored pens, crayons, and colored pencils available for them to use. Markers are not a good idea since they will bleed through to the other side of the page.

PARTICIPATING AND PREPARING FOR ADDITIONAL READING WORK

In a well-established reading workshop, you'll find a buzz of activity in full swing across the independent reading portion. In addition to quality time alone engaged in self-selected texts, your workshop may include a variety of additional learning opportunities that showcase other ways your students can put reading into action. For example, children may also spend time during independent reading preparing for or meeting with book clubs, working with their research groups and writing up their findings, following up on remaining tasks from their small group work, crafting a book talk for later, or even doing some reflective writing about their goals established during their individual conferences.

When we give students the time to work on responses, prepare for a reading conversation, or get lost in reading, we indicate that this work is important. What we make time for shows what we value. Dedicating our precious classroom time to the independent work of reading workshop will show children that reading is something we value and a gift we want to give them. We'll take a closer look at several of these options in the chapter that follows.

What Are the Teachers Doing During Independent Reading?

During independent reading time, teachers are just as busy and focused on their readers, circling the room, meeting with individuals and groups, and keeping a watch for ways they can support students toward greater levels of responsibility for their reading. While some teachers like to begin independent reading time by reading from their own books to model that they are a lifelong reader too, we find it more valuable to spend this precious time with students in small-group instruction and reading conferences. To help set a tone of independence, teachers often transition from the minilesson to independent reading in an intentional way by conducting a status of the class.

STATUS OF THE CLASS

We learned about status of the class in Nancie Atwell's *The Reading Zone, Second Edition: How to Help Kids Become Skilled, Passionate, Habitual, Critical Readers* (2016) and in Donalyn Miller's *Reading in the Wild: The Book Whisperer's Keys to Cultivating Lifelong Reading Habits* (2014). This formative assessment routine can help teachers easily track how their readers are spending their independent reading time. Before independent reading time, call on each of your students to give you the title of the book they are reading and the page number. You will record the date, an "F" if they have *finished* a book, an "A" if they have *abandoned* a book, an "S" if they are ready to *start* a new book, or a "C" if they are ready for a *conference* with you. You might also add an "R" for *recommends* this book as a way to encourage other readers in the class to try it out! In three or four minutes, you know what all your students are reading! This information can help you praise students who are completing a book and encourage students who are moving slowly. You might want to check in with those students who are not finishing a book for a long period of time to see if you can offer support. This daily record helps you communicate with your students about the books they are reading, perhaps by suggesting a book that is less challenging but about the same topic, or helping them explore a new genre. It also provides some accountability for making good use of daily independent reading time. Students expect that they will report ("share out") in a whole-group discussion, a gentle way to raise the level of participation without a great deal of stress. The status of the class roll call will reveal your readers' preferences and let other students hear what everyone else is reading—providing possibilities for future reads.

KIDWATCHING

During the first six to ten minutes of independent reading time, everyone is silent. You'll spend most of this time observing students' readerly behavior and noting it while you are "clipboard cruising." This kidwatching (Goodman and Owocki 2002) can help you gather information about students' progress, understanding, strengths and challenges, cooperation, reading habits, and attitude. As you circulate, you can observe students who are flipping back to reread or who are staring at one page for a long period of time. Some readers may jot notes or write in their response journals. You may notice certain students who move quickly through their piles of selected books, from one to the other, without ever really reading any of them. Others will be deeply engrossed in one book and stay with it all week or even for a two-week period until it is finished. You may see some students engaged in "fake reading"—simply turning pages to be compliant—while others "read" the illustrations and text features. Jot these important observations on sticky notes and transfer them to an electronic file or notebook when you have a chance, preferably that same day. This kidwatching leads to the important work you'll do to differentiate instruction during independent reading time—the work of conferring and feedback.

CONFERRING WITH STUDENTS

Independent reading during reading workshop includes the idea that students should have conversations about the books they are reading, and some of the most impactful conversations your students will have will

happen one-on-one with you during reading conferences. The purposes of a reading conference are many: to encourage and grow readers, to manage instruction, to discover interests, to promote reflection, to formatively assess students' progress, and to set new reading goals. Laura Robb (1998) suggests that conferences build students' confidence because they allow students to talk about and practice a strategy they have been taught. When teachers give their undivided attention to a child in a one-on-one conference, the student feels you care about their learning and want them to understand and improve. To support these conversations, we prefer that students bring their reading response journals to share summaries, reflections, and other notes, including thumbnail sketches of characters, setting, and more. Reading conferences are highly productive both in terms of instruction and in providing valuable information for instruction. For example, patterns identified through a teacher's collection of conference notes might prompt a minilesson focus on fluency, vocabulary, or comprehension for the entire class. We suggest reviewing your conference notes several times a week to look for areas where explicit instruction or a review of important concepts would be beneficial.

Figure 7.6 During a one-on-one conference with a student, Brenda assesses how he uses written response to clarify his thinking about a text.

In addition, reading conferences are a great time to help readers set short-term and long-term goals. During this up-close time, teachers can analyze reading behaviors related to sustaining the reading process as they determine what strategic actions students are taking to solve words, monitor and correct reading, search for and use information, adjust reading rate, and summarize narratives and informational pieces. They can determine how readers are using systems of strategic actions introduced during minilessons while students are independently reading. In a reading conference, teachers can monitor for or prompt students to try out strategic actions offered in the day's minilesson or from several collective minilessons about a specific strategic action. For example, students can be encouraged to try making predictions, making connections, inferring, synthesizing, asking questions, clarifying, and analyzing. On a higher level, this focused time allows for deeper interactions that will help students become critical readers, using information from a text to think about critical literacy-social issues, world issues, human problems, gender, and cultural bias.

You can conduct roving conferences, sitting right next to your readers wherever they are seated in the classroom. Invite them to share what they are thinking and/or feeling about what they are reading, and take notes. Ask exploratory questions like, "What was the most interesting part of the book so far? Why?"; "Is this book a good choice for you? Why or why not?"; and "Have you read this author before? What are you discovering about this author? Will you choose another book he/she has written? The same genre?" Here is a brief process to guide you that will help make conferring one-on-one with your readers more successful (see **Appendices F** and **H** for even more ideas):

1. Listen to the reader. You may have them retell what they have been reading, offer an opinion, share something from their response journal, or ask for specific help about how to navigate a new genre or use a strategy that was introduced in the last minilesson.
2. Using what you heard, make a decision about what to talk about with this reader, offering specific praise for what you notice them doing and then teaching something new.
3. Teach the reader something that will help them move forward as a reader.
4. Use discussion points you've prepared in advance to address the student's present goal.

5. Help the reader craft a reading goal or decide to continue with the present goal.

KEEPING TRACK

There is no magical formula for keeping conference notes, but finding a process that works for you is the key. Consider what you want to recall and what seems most manageable. Often, during a conference, we note a variety of things we might teach readers. Some teachers find it helpful to organize these notes into two columns—one for dated notes and the other to translate those notes into possible minilessons for the whole group, opportunities to extend learning through small group instruction, or future individual reading goals. Other options include jotting your thoughts on sticky notes or mailing labels and then transferring them to a central location later in the day. Brenda prefers to use a notebook with a page for each student. Her notes include a date, the book discussed, observations, teaching suggestions, and goals for the next meeting. Brenda also sketches out two or three possible teaching points, prioritizes the most pressing one, teaches it, and then dates it to indicate what was taught during the conference. Regardless of the method that works best for you, keeping track is ultimately a way to help you translate your conferences and observations with students into the next, right step for them as readers.

Video 7.3 ▶

Independent Reading in a First Grade Classroom

Children settle in and read around the room during independent reading workshop.

Figure 7.7 In a primary reading workshop, readers often read many books during workshop. Notice the additional books spread out on this young first grader's desk.

Figure 7.8 During independent reading, Brenda moves around the classroom to observe and listen in as partners read their books to each other.

Final Thoughts

We value reading. As readers ourselves, we look for extended times to sit and read. This is something we strive to give our students in the workshop setting. But this time is more than that; it is an important instructional time in our day. Through the use of small group instruction and reading conferences, we connect with the children in our room and give them important strategies they can use to become independent readers. In reading workshop, independent reading time offers more than just reading time. In a workshop approach, you will see teachers observing the readerly behavior of their students, conferring, and offering feedback. You may see them interrupt readers to deliver a mid-workshop teaching point or offer praise to spur them on. Teachers will sometimes guide the book selection, monitor use of skills and strategies, teach small groups, hold roving conferences, and help their readers set goals. This independent reading time is the heart of the workshop.

Stop and Reflect

1. How do you know when students are pretending to read during independent reading time? What do you do to help them become more engaged readers—what are some ways to get students really reading?

2. How effective are the notes you take during your conferences? What are some manageable ways you can keep helpful information on your readers and put those notes to use to plan your next level of instruction?

Something to Try

Ask a colleague to videotape some of your reading conferences (you can offer to do the same for them) and review them to evaluate how you're doing and where you might make a few changes.

Chapter 8

Small Group Work: Safe Environments to Share Thinking and Build Confidence

Differentiated reading instruction is best attained through flexible, purposeful groupings and attention to the repertoire of ways to meet students' needs.

– **Jennifer Serravallo,**
Teaching Reading in Small Groups: Differentiating
Instruction for Building Strategic, Independent Readers

Mr. Telford calls together Joel, Katie, and Jordan. They meet on the carpet in a tight circle with their independent reading books and their reader's notebooks. Mr. Telford has decided to work with these three readers because of information he has gained by observing them during the minilesson and through his conferences. He has noted that these students are ready to read books where dialogue is not always tagged and wants to help these readers navigate these types of texts. He begins the group lesson by stating his purpose.

"Today I want to teach you a strategy you can use to help you recognize who is talking in the text." He uses a demonstration text, in this case *The SOS File* (2004) by Betsy Byars, Betsy Duffey, and Laurie Myers, to illustrate how dialogue is not always tagged and then he shows how he determines who is speaking. He reads from the beginning of the chapter entitled "The Chocolate SOS." "Notice how the author doesn't say who is talking directly," he tells the students, "but drops in clues." He reads:

> I said, "Mom, I need to borrow forty dollars. Please don't ask me what I need it for."
>
> "What do you need it for?"
>
> I knew she would say that.
>
> "Please, just give me the money. I'll work it off somehow."
>
> "You cannot expect me to hand over forty dollars. What have you done?"
>
> "Please, Mom."
>
> "What have you done?"

Mr. Telford demonstrates a strategy for determining who is speaking—noticing when a new paragraph begins and looking for introductory phrases, pronouns, and proper nouns. "Now, look in your books for dialogue and see if you can determine who is speaking."

The three begin reading quietly from their own texts and Mr. Telford leans in to Katie. She points to the text and explains how she determined who is talking by following the paragraphs and writing the speaker's initials in places to help her. Mr. Telford commends her thinking, writes something on a sticky note for her, and moves to Joel and Jordan, who each need a different level of instructional support to successfully use this strategy.

Afterward, the group refocuses and Mr. Telford revisits the strategy, encouraging them to use it as they read. Mr. Telford has prepared sticky notes with simple reminders of what they discussed to place in their notebooks. The group disbands. Mr. Telford checks his watch. The entire lesson took less than ten minutes. He makes simple notes for himself and moves on to confer with some individual readers.

Why Use Small Group Instruction?

During independent reading time, you might notice that—like Mr. Telford—you have a handful of students who could use some time together working on the same concept. Small group time during the reading workshop offers a different level of instruction and conversation than readers will encounter during the whole group minilesson or individual conferences and has a significant impact on student achievement (Hattie, 2009). With its reduced teacher-to-student ratio, small group instruction can personalize learning, giving time for you to interact with each student in the group: listening, responding, questioning, and evaluating. Sometimes, students are selected for small group instruction based on an immediate need, such as how to apply reading skills when reading digitally. Other small groups may form to review and extend a strategy learned during the minilesson, such as how to infer or how to read infographics. These small groups usually last about ten to fifteen minutes in time. In other instances, you might call a group together to review and reinforce a strategy by presenting it in a different setting (e.g., its use in nonfiction work as opposed to its use with fiction texts) or extend it for those students who are ready for more. Note that small group instruction doesn't have to always be about teaching something new. It can also be about reteaching a skill or strategy through a new lens. In addition, a small group can give teachers a place to pre-teach specific vocabulary, reinforce sound–spelling relationships and how to use those relationships to read words, introduce new text structures, or frontload prerequisite knowledge for students who may experience challenges in upcoming lessons. Small group instruction ensures increased instructional time, increased peer interaction, increased engagement, and opportunities for teachers to explicitly teach a skill and check for understanding.

A key aspect of small groups in the reading workshop is that they are flexible. They can include a quick check-in or be spread out for multiple opportunities for slow and deliberate study. Groups can meet regularly or members can move in and out of them based on their growth and needs. According to Shubitz and Dorfman (2019), "flexible grouping organizes students intentionally and fluidly for different learning experiences over a relatively short period of time" (123). We agree! This brevity is imperative. Remember, small groups are flexible and fluid—never permanent assignments lasting the entire school year. Flexible grouping helps us to re-energize our workshop as students interact with different peers, practice successful reading behaviors, and come to realize that everyone is a teacher and a learner in a community of readers.

Figure 8.1 Emma listens as Brenda offers feedback to her question about taking notes on the compare/contrast nonfiction structure using a Venn diagram.

An overall goal for small group work is to help students move on to more increasingly challenging texts by reading strategically and fluently. At the end of small group instruction time, students return to their work as independent readers, often trying out the new learning with their chosen text. This is another benefit of small group instruction work. There is an underlying expectation that students will practice the concept they have explored as they gain the knowledge and the confidence to try it on their own.

What Is Reading Workshop?

Reading workshop is a framework for reading instruction that combines teacher and student actions and interactions that provide agency and independent choice and voice so students are confident, lifelong, successful readers. Structures within the workshop include: Read-Aloud, Shared Reading, Interactive Reading, Guided Reading, Independent Reading, Conferencing, and Book Groups that provide the appropriate mix of whole group, small group, and individual work that culminates in success. Skills and strategies allow students to demonstrate their command of the reading components: phonemic awareness, phonics, fluency, vocabulary, and comprehension as they show evidence of deep thinking, critical analysis, and synthesis of ideas as demonstrated in writing, speaking, and listening.

Fran McVeigh,
Independent literacy consultant and blogger

The central benefits to small group instruction is that every student is engaged and everyone has a voice. The time in small group provides opportunities for students to have age-appropriate conversations that can stretch their thinking. Small group work allows teachers to teach strategies and organizational structures *before* and *during* the reading process as well. Providing structure allows us to see the big picture and helps our students know what to expect, but we also need flexibility to allow us to be responsive to students' immediate needs and to make changes without disrupting the flow of the workshop. Small group instruction allows us to provide routine, but at the same time maintain flexibility to best meet student needs at any given time in the school year.

How Do You Determine Who Is in a Small Group?

Small group instruction begins with a determination of what is to be taught and to whom. Using daily observation, anecdotal records, conference notes, and other informal (as well as formal) assessments, you can create a small group (three to five students) around any particular instructional need. Even an exit slip can be used for upper elementary and middle school students to quickly assess who still has questions and who might be ready for enrichment and extensions. As you continue to monitor in formal and informal ways, readers can be grouped and regrouped by shared need as flexibly and as often as you like. For instance, calling together a group of students who have experienced difficulty with the concept taught in your minilesson immediately after you taught the lesson can be a way to remediate, offer more explicit instruction, or just give more guided practice to some students. Or, you could just as easily form a cooperative group of students with diverse abilities to work collaboratively based on an interest.

TEACHER TIP: Since you likely won't always meet with each student in a small group every week, keeping a weekly list of who you meet with and why will help you keep track of the work you're doing with readers in small groups.

When Is It Time for Small Group Instruction?

During small group instruction, with your support, students engage with and briefly practice a skill just taught to them. This gives you an indication of whether the students may need to meet again for more instruction in the next several days. You have a lot of choice in deciding when to hold a small group meeting. Deciding on the purpose of the group will help you determine when to meet with your group (see **Figure 8.2**). The flexibility of the workshop format allows you to choose a group-meeting time that will be most beneficial for the group.

Figure 8.2 If/then chart to decide when to hold your group

If . . .	Then . . .
you are using this time to pre-teach a skill or strategy to offer support for readers who may struggle with the concept . . .	consider holding this group before the mini-lesson or a day before teaching the concept to the whole group.
you'll be reinforcing a concept previously taught and giving more time for guided practice . . .	consider holding this group after the mini-lesson or after holding conferences with 2 to 5 readers to allow readers more time to practice the concept independently before checking in with them.
this group is meeting for remedial work or if this group needs to have the mini-lesson retaught . . .	consider holding this group immediately following the mini-lesson to continue the teaching you have already started.
the students need to revisit or expand on important procedures that need to become familiar, such as how to set club goals for a book club group or how to use sticky notes in different ways (such as coding with a simple system such as Q is for question and I is for inference) . . .	consider bringing this group together right before they'll have to implement the procedure, or as you see the need to practice or review a procedure arise in real time.
this group is meeting for enrichment purposes such as expanding their learning about a genre or a literacy concept such as the use of foreshadowing in fiction . . .	consider interest and research groups as a great way to extend learning or capitalize on student curiosity. These enrichment groups can meet any time and can work independent of you.

One helpful hint about scheduling small groups: remember to save time in your workshop so you can confer with readers and so students who meet as a group also have time to read independently. It is easy to get caught up in teaching a group and watch your conferring time (and their reading time) diminish or run out! We recommend leading just one or two small groups daily so you will still have enough time available to meet with

individual readers for conferences. If you have multiple groups running, remember that most groups don't need to meet daily or even more than once a week. Keeping your schedule flexible will also leave you time to form, in the moment, small groups as the needs arise.

Figure 8.3 Brenda uses different colored sticky notes to make it easier to manage groups and students during independent reading. The notes make it easier to be flexible in scheduling.

> **TEACHER TIP:** Remember, while you're working with small groups, the rest of the class is going about the business of independent reading—reading to themselves, working with partners, exploring with interest or research groups, or tending to procedural needs.

Types of Small Group Instruction

In this section, we suggest various formats for small group instruction that will help you meet the diverse needs of the readers in your community. A variety of formats allows for greater flexibility. After all, small group instruction benefits everyone, not just your striving readers. We take a bit more time to discuss guided reading and book clubs in order to provide more of the nuts and bolts you'll need to implement those specific formats successfully.

STRATEGY GROUP

A strategy group focuses on a specific strategy a group of students needs at a particular time. These readers may not all be reading the same book or even working on the same reading level. For example, a group might meet three times to work on inferring a character trait based on a character's actions or absence of actions. The teacher offers explicit instruction on the use of the skill or strategy, often through demonstration and modeling, giving the group a glimpse into how the strategy can be used. Then each student has time to practice the strategy and receive specific feedback while reading their individually chosen book before the teacher moves on to the next student in the group.

Figure 8.4

This flexible group meets together with their teacher to learn a reading strategy. After their teacher demonstrates, each child practices using the strategy with their independent reading book.

INSTRUCTIONAL LEVEL GROUPS

At times it may be beneficial to call a group of readers together to work on navigating texts on a specific level with more ease. This type of group is perfect for students who could benefit from working their way through books with similar features or challenges. Level groups might be incorporated to aid students who are ready to move up a level, or a way to help students as they begin a more complex level. When building this type of group, it's important to keep in mind that reading levels are approximations and often fluctuate based on students' reading behaviors as well as their interest and background knowledge related to a topic. These groups should remain flexible.

ON-THE-RUN GROUPS

Some small groups are formed in the moment as the teacher moves around the room conferring and observing the class. For example, you notice several students with the same misconception or encounter a small group that could use immediate feedback on a skill or strategy. This type of group is great for addressing those teachable moments that pop up while you're clipboard cruising, because an on-the-run group can be immediately formed to meet student needs in real time. Keeping track of who you worked with and what you taught will provide valuable information for planning future conferences and minilesson topics, as well as possibilities for readers you might follow up with in future strategy groups.

GENRE-BASED GROUPS

Genre-based groups meet so the teacher can offer background on how to navigate a genre or to teach strategies that reading a particular genre requires. This could be fiction or nonfiction. Imagine bringing together a small group of mystery readers. Do they understand how the author sets the reader up with early clues to uncover the mystery in the first few chapters? Will they need help navigating who are "suspects" and which events are important? What strategies could you suggest that will help

them keep track of clues and their thinking along the way? Maybe this group is ready to stretch their thinking about mysteries and explore the meaning of a red herring, false clues planted to build tension and distract readers. Or perhaps you have noticed a group reading nonfiction that needs help understanding how to navigate a text filled with sidebars, graphs, maps, photographs, and captions laden with information? Do they have a purpose for reading? Will they need strategies for taking and sharing notes? What will they do with this new information? These types of groups change as the readers move in and out of genres.

RESEARCH GROUPS

One way to share research skills is through small-group instruction based on students' interests and/or needs. Students will often form their own research groups around an essential question they want to explore, or you can nudge them to figure something new out together. Initially, you may need to teach them how to take field notes, write detailed observations, cite material, or use electronic resources that support online learning. But, once you give students the tools to research, you can step back and let them dig in! Then, you can check in with them when they need your help but give them the freedom to explore and decide how they will share their findings with the rest of the class. For more, be sure to read *Inquiry Illuminated: Researcher's Workshop across the Curriculum* by Goudvis, Harvey, and Buhrow (2019).

GUIDED READING GROUPS

A guided reading group is usually called together to work on a specific comprehension skill, for word study, for decoding practice, or for a specific reading behavior using the same text. Guided reading is important throughout the elementary grades. At the primary level, the focus is on developing phonemic awareness, phonics skills, and fluency and connecting that work directly to making meaning. At the intermediate level, guided reading groups focus more on applying specific comprehension skills and strategies and the processing of large amounts of text. Children read the text silently and reread aloud to find specific passages to support their responses to discussion questions. The teacher may listen as each child reads a paragraph or two from the selected text to observe word-solving strategies and evaluate fluency issues. While they do this, the rest of the children continue to read silently. The teacher will have a signal to indicate to the child that they are to begin reading aloud and a signal for them to stop and continue reading silently.

One important quality of a guided reading lesson is that it moves swiftly from one component to the next and relies on effective organization and quick thinking on your part to do well. In time, you'll learn a format and process that works best for you, but **Figure 8.5** includes a glimpse at a typical format to give you an idea.

There is a handover of responsibility in a guided reading lesson. According to Routman (2018), "what is key is that students are expected to do the majority of the thinking and strategizing in this guided practice, learning stage" (219). This sets them up for success during independent reading where, Routman notes, students get a chance to "put on the miles" as readers during reading workshop time. It is here that students take the learning acquired in guided reading groups and use that learning to successfully read and comprehend on their own, extending the teaching and learning experiences to other reading experiences across the day.

Figure 8.5 Guided reading lesson format

Selecting a text	Select a text that will introduce and/or reinforce the concepts your students need to work on.
Word work/vocabulary	Select high-impact words worth studying closely to support ongoing phonics work in the curriculum or specific student decoding needs in the text at hand. This is a great time to explore spelling patterns and multiple meanings of words.
Introduce the text	Lead a picture walk or help readers make a connection to the author, topic, or genre and discuss the title. Make predictions about the content.
Reading the text	Students read silently as you listen to individual readers read a portion of the text aloud to check decoding strategies and fluency or lead quick instructional moments.
Discussing the text	Give students time to talk while you listen and make some notes. Guide them to talk about the meaning of the text by providing them with prompts to help them focus the discussion and engage with meaningful responses.
Teaching the strategy	Use 3–5 minutes to introduce, teach, or reinforce a skill/strategy you have taught as preparation for use during independent reading and across the day in content areas.
Extending meaning (optional)	Students write about the reading to extend their understanding of the text. This response could be about personal connections, opinions, and/or relevant themes.
Word work (optional)	In addition to leading word work during the introduction, you may consider doing some additional word work after the text is discussed.

Guided reading groups can offer remediation or enrichment, but remember to keep all your groups fluid and flexible, changing as your readers grow and take on new reading challenges.

Figure 8.6 Sometimes small groups are *small*. Not all students need the same skills and strategies at the same time.

BOOK CLUBS

Just as in the adult world, book clubs allow students to enjoy reading as a social activity. But, on top of that, you'll find loads of teaching potential in this particular small group format. When we listen in and take notes, we notice group members implementing skills and strategies while being exposed to peers' thinking as they discuss a book. In a book club, children grow more empathetic and compassionate as they learn to listen to and respond with respect to ideas that may be different from their own and to think differently about topics they may not have spent time considering before. For instance, one book club in Brenda's third grade class read a variety of picture books about children who were struggling with getting daily needs: food, clothing, and shelter. This led to a discussion on the amounts of food they saw wasted in the cafeteria. The book club decided to take action and made posters to hang in the school cafeteria to encourage children to place food on a "share" table for others to eat instead of throwing it out.

Preparing for Book Clubs

Book club preparation begins early on with read-alouds that embrace student responses and encourage lively discussions. Before our young readers embark on leading their own book clubs, we begin teaching them conversational moves that allow all student voices to be heard. Using an interactive read-aloud introduces the class to a variety of ways to interact with a text, their peers, and their teacher (Serravallo, 2010). Planning for these interactive read-alouds is very important, because it helps you deliberately model language and conversational moves that will establish expectations for the ways readers in your community think and respond together. Adding your own sticky notes to indicate where you will stop and share your thinking with the students will help you be more efficient with your use of time and keep you from wandering from the strategy/skill/author move you are highlighting. You may ask your students to stop and jot, turn and talk with a partner, or share their thinking with the whole group. Taking time to teach children to listen and respond will help them carry these important habits over to their club time. Take your time; the more prep work and modeling, the more success you will see in clubs!

Video 8.1 ▶

Book Club in a Third Grade Classroom

Third graders discuss a book using strategies they have learned to keep conversations going and reference the text.

Figure 8.7 Third graders use a text set to talk about spiders. One third grader shares information from his text to help make his point clear to his club members.

TEACHER TIP: Just before you launch book clubs, establish book club groups that sit together during your interactive read-aloud so they can get in the habit of interacting with their club during whole group turn-and-talks. While the children practice listening and responding, you can listen to their conversations for potential minilessons that will help them be successful once they're off on their own.

Organizing for Book Clubs

A book club begins with children selecting the text they want to read and setting goals for the group. Allowing children to choose the text they want to read can ensure greater engagement and interest in the text and the group. Of course, you don't want to overdo it, but as the teacher you can also nudge readers toward book choices that can be simultaneously used to meet your instructional needs. Perhaps your book clubs will read texts with a focus on character studies, or maybe your curriculum asks you to teach a unit of study in historical fiction or biography. It makes perfect sense to go win-win here and select texts that will lend to this study and match the readers in your book clubs.

Some book clubs are created organically as children read books together. In Brenda's third grade class a group of readers decided they were going to read *The Doll People* by Ann Martin and Laura Goodwin in a club. The group created reading assignments, wrote thoughts in their notebooks, and met together to discuss their thinking. Watching the club and its interactions allowed Brenda to see reading skills and strategies in action and note ways to push these readers forward into deeper comprehension and discussion skills.

TEACHER TIP: Book selection is important for the success of book clubs but, sometimes, kids need a little guidance in this area. You can scaffold this by highlighting three to five books and book talking them to the whole class. Allow students the opportunity to look through the books and do some skimming. Then, invite readers to write a note to you to indicate their choice of first or second book choice.

Getting the Conversation Started and Keeping It Going

When book clubs first meet, you might notice a lag in the energy as readers who normally have lots to say seem to struggle with how to kick things off. This is when a good scaffold can really help. For the first few club meetings, we like to suggest students jot down key questions in their response journals so they can come prepared to activate a thoughtful, engaging discussion (see **Figure 8.8**). You might provide them with some questions on a handout to get them started or perhaps create questions on an anchor chart together with your students. This initial support is best when presented as open-ended questions that elicit myriad responses that are rich and varied. Though you'll find some students don't need this level of support, many will be glad to have it until they get in the swing of things, and still others will need to refer back to it periodically when things come to a lull.

Figure 8.8

Book Club Guiding Questions

1 What is the text about?
2 What parts do you especially like?
3 What suggestions, questions, or comments would you have for the author?
4 How can you present a key idea from this text to your classmates?
5 What is/are the theme(s)? What evidence can you provide?

Another way to support book club conversations is to help students to decide how many pages/chapters they will read at the end of each book club meeting and think about how they'll prepare to share their thinking with the group the next time they meet. Help them understand the importance of supporting their talking points with evidence from the text. Perhaps you can suggest they place sticky notes on pages where they will want to cite or quote directly from the text. Finally, help your students think about questions that will lead to self-evaluation. Am I supporting and contributing to my book club's discussion? How so? Did I use the text to support my thoughts? Did I stay focused on the conversation? Did I listen attentively to my peers' responses and respond in an appropriate and supporting manner?

Maintaining Book Club Discussions

As readers gain more confidence in their book cub conversations, protocols can raise the bar, helping promote a healthy spirit of collaboration as well as more substantive conversations through rich discussions and shared responses to reading. Protocols are simply guidelines for conversation based on norms that everyone agrees upon in order to support safe and effective dialog. For instance, a simple discussion guide like the one in **Figure 8.9** might be created with the students and posted for all to see and refer to throughout their book club experiences. We believe that keeping it simple is the best way to ensure that all the students will use the guidelines successfully. For more protocols to adopt or adapt for use with your book clubs, see **Appendix G: Protocols for Book Club and Small Group Discussion**.

Figure 8.9

Discussion Guidelines Chart

A   Stick to the topic.

B   Pay attention to the person talking.

C   Ask questions about ideas given.

D   Give everyone a chance to participate.

E   Try not to interrupt others.

Assessing Student Work in Book Clubs

How do I know what they are doing if I am not "in charge," and how do I assess their work? For many teachers, these are important questions that, if left unanswered, leave them wary of giving book clubs a try. But don't let that hesitation stop you. It's true, you can't always be with a book club. But you can follow their progress in a variety of ways that build your confidence over time that learning is, in fact, happening when your students are given space to take the lead.

Consider collecting the club's reader's notebooks after a session. How are they responding? Are they just retelling or are they thinking more deeply about the text? Or, have students write a letter to you in their notebooks about their thinking and the work they have been doing in book clubs. Consider writing back, responding to the reader's comments first and then purposefully modeling something you think the reader could attempt and pass on to the other club members. Can you record the book club and listen to it later? Could the group make a visual representation of their thinking? Individual conferences are also a great place to discuss how members think their book club work is going and where they need help or guidance. It is also a time you might introduce something to an individual club member that they could teach their club.

TEACHER TIP: Ask each member of a book club to write one sentence about their book club learning on a sticky note, with their name, and collect them at the completion of club time. Use different color sticky notes for different purposes; for example, blue for *Today I learned* . . . ; red for *Help, our group needs help with* . . . , or *We are confused about* . . . ; yellow for *Our group is really good at* . . . . You can read them later and make comments or use the information for future lessons.

One way to assess the effectiveness of your book clubs is to consider your original intentions. Look around. How are the book clubs going? Are you able to observe improvement in the way the students interact, the kinds of questions they ask, the ways they offer reflection? Are they able to "keep the volleyball in the air" for longer periods of time—that is, are they able to layer the talk, piggybacking on each other's responses and adding important details as evidence for their opinions? Do you observe the tracks of your teaching in their book club discussions and written responses? Are you noticing students talking about craft moves, using inference to read between the lines, visualization, and summary strategies, and asking questions that engage their club members in higher order thinking skills? Are readers using literary tools like elements of story (plot, conflict, setting, character, resolution, theme) to enhance their discussion instead of spending most of their time in retellings? Are you looking for evidence that group members continue to grow their reading identities through book club interactions? Do you see them taking risks and trying new things so they can grow as readers? What kinds of risks can you document—trying out a new genre, choosing more challenging texts, spending more time reading, sharing their thinking on a regular basis?

One final note here. You may be tempted to ask kids in book clubs to create an artificial project when they complete the book, but consider this—when was the last time you created a diorama or wrote a skit at the completion of reading a book? Stephanie Harvey and Harvey Daniels (2009) remind us that as adults we don't rush to "make" something when we finish a book; instead, we move to talk about it. They urge us to make reading responses authentic so "we don't assign an arbitrary or superficial project at the end of each book. Instead we ask, 'How has this book changed you in some way? Where does this book take you next? What do you want to find out or do as a result of reading this? Do you have any lingering questions?'" (203). Consider asking book club members to use similar questions to initiate a group conversation or offer individual or shared written responses on the class's book blog as way to assess their thinking.

What If I have Some Students That Do Not Want to Participate in a Book Club?

We have to always keep our overarching goal in mind—we want to increase readership in our classroom and help students enjoy reading. Increasing a student's anxiety level or fostering a negative attitude about reading is what we hope to avoid. If students are resistant to joining in with book clubs, Dr. Sonja Cherry-Paul and Dana Johansen, the authors of *Breathing New Life Into Book Clubs: A Practical Guide for Teachers* (2019), suggest that we offer another option—perhaps continuing to read independently and checking in with us in a one-to-one conference or reading with a trusted partner. We stay cautious here. We want these students to decide on their own to participate in book clubs offered during the latter part of the year— and they likely won't do that if they're forced to participate early on.

Figure 8.10 These students wanted to read about butterflies but couldn't find other members for their book club, so they created a partnership instead. Allowing students this option gives choice and ownership in the process.

Keeping Notes During Small Group Instruction

Keeping track of who you've worked with and what you've worked on can make or break small group instruction, so finding a system that works for you is key. Just as in other kidwatching examples, sometimes we find the simplest way to take notes is to write one or two observations on a sticky note. Then, you can transfer your notes to a larger notebook with pages dedicated for each student in the class in alphabetical order for easier access. You might even place them in three columns—one to tape sticky notes, another for your critical thoughts about the observation, and the last column to imagine future instruction. Be creative and flexible as you develop your management system for keeping notes. If you are not comfortable with your system you are not likely to use it, so take some time to rethink things as needed. Another great idea is to survey your colleagues. What works best for them? Ask them to share the ways they keep track of their small groups and what everyone is learning. Here are some general tips to think about as you consider what system will work best for you:

- Initially, organize information from what you actually see and hear. Do not include your thoughts and feelings. Keep it clean and simple! Later, you will analyze your observations.

- Keep focused and stay engaged on the task at hand.

- Listen more; talk less.

- Write down what students can do so instructional decisions are based on children's strengths. For example, Jesse can recall details so she is ready to state the main idea.

- Take a photo of student work or behavior to add to an anecdotal record.

- Think critically about what you are observing while you are observing it.

- Draw conclusions and identify areas of need (concern).

- Use abbreviations to capture detailed observations in an efficient way.

- Be prepared to reread your notes and use them to form new groups, adjust the groups you presently have, and refocus instruction by addressing any areas of concern. Recognize that these notes are for you and your reflection. Consider adapting your notes for clarity if you want to share them with caregivers or administrators.

Figure 8.11

An Example of a Note-Taking Chart

Student's Name: _Jaime W._   Week: 1 2 ③ 4 5 6 7 8 9

Strategy/Skill	Observation	Notes	Fluency
Participating in a discussion about the story	Restates what someone else has said. Not yet initiating original thinking.	Ready to piggy-back on ideas voiced by peers ("I agree with ___ because ..."; "I can add to ___'s thoughts about ...").	(+ √ + √ -) +

There are many effective ways to organize your small group notes. In this chart, four columns are used to note the strategy, what was observed, a quick reflection, and an easy way to indicate fluency competency.

Final Thoughts

Small group instruction enhances your reading community by increasing peer interaction time and building students' confidence to share their thinking. It gives us increased instructional time and more opportunities for students to work together on shared goals and improve on targeted skills and strategies from previous minilessons. Whether through teacher-led groups like strategy groups or guided reading or independent student groups like book clubs or research groups, this setting makes room for learners to practice their interpersonal and leadership skills and grow into readers who will read beyond their classroom experiences. Through discussion and reflection, they will be able to imagine ways to carry their new learning into their future reading work. The knowledge and newfound confidence will help these students read with enthusiasm and interest.

Stop and Reflect

1. How will you manage your time in a given week to tuck in small group instruction in ways that make the most sense for you and your students?
2. Consider the various types of small groups discussed in this chapter. What types of groups might you offer your current students? Who would benefit the most?

Something to Try

Keeping track of students in small groups can be challenging. Try one of our suggestions for note-taking or create something for yourself. Use this tool for a few weeks and evaluate its effectiveness.

Chapter 9

Sharing and Reflection: Building Trust and Respect for Each Other's Ideas

Reflecting on experiences encourages insight and complex learning. We foster our own growth when we control our learning, so some reflection is best done alone. Reflection is also enhanced, however, when we ponder our learning with others.

– Art L. Costa and Bena Callick,
Learning and Leading with Habits of Mind

Jacob and Nathan are sitting next to Ms. Teel on the black cubes by the chart stand that displays what was taught during the minilesson; it's an anchor chart showing one way to take notes when reading a sequentially structured nonfiction text. The class gathers. "Today readers, you read nonfiction texts and tried to take notes using a list. You numbered the information in a list to show the sequential steps. Tell the person sitting next to you what you learned in your reading." The children turn and begin to give factual details in sequential order. Ms. Teel continues, "I could hear your facts and saw many of you use your fingers to say *first, next, then* . . . . Jacob and Nathan are going to share their notebooks and their work today." She turns to them and they hold up their notebooks, showing their lists, but then something unexpected happens.

Jacob begins, "We used the list when we started but then we thought, this text is about the life cycle of a frog. Cycle . . . Get it? A circle. It doesn't end at the bottom of the list, it goes back to the beginning and starts all over again."

"Yeah," chimes in Nathan. They are now visibly excited, standing up and taking on a teaching posture. "So we had to change it." Nathan looks at Ms. Teel, almost apologetically, but with great pride. "Now our notes look like this." The boys move from the chart stand to the white board and begin drawing their cycle. They explain how they created this cycle, and why it makes sense to use this graphic when the sequence of information is a cycle. Ms. Teel nods and smiles. They conclude to a round of applause, as she begins adjusting tomorrow's minilesson plans in her head.

Why Are Share Sessions So Important?

Though we normally see them used to close the reading workshop, share sessions can actually occur any time and are an important way to engage in purposeful conversations about reading while building community. A truly versatile component of the reading workshop, these sessions can take a variety of formats and serve a multitude of purposes (see **Figure 9.1**). For instance, many share sessions occur in whole group format, but they can also be adjusted so that students share their journal entries with a partner while the other person gives feedback. Other times, students might document their thinking in a gallery walk format that allows for quick displays of everyone's individual thinking. Share sessions can invite readers to share their thinking orally or in creative, written ways, and can showcase student responses, processes, or success with newly learned reading behaviors.

Often, as we allow children to take the lead and invite them to share their thinking and strategies, a share session can take a delightful turn, with the students becoming the teacher in the room. In this way, the share

becomes its own minilesson as readers detail their use of processes and their strategy success stories with the community. Peter Johnston (2012) reminds us to "make sure that students know how to teach one another. We need to help them become lifelong teachers as well as lifelong learners" (50). The share session is great place to start.

Overall, share sessions link the work students do in reading workshop to speaking, listening, and writing and—because of this—can also provide opportunities for ongoing formative assessment. In *Teaching with Intention* (2008), Debbie Miller suggests that we take notes when our students are sharing and reflecting and then take the time to study them because it is one of the best measures of what our students understand. You may even choose to document student thinking during share time by creating an anchor chart while they're sharing.

Share sessions help students build trust and respect for each other's ideas and establish routines for accountable talk, so the time you spend in them is just as important to the reading workshop as the minilesson and independent reading time. Share sessions don't have to be long, but please, don't skip them! However you decide to create pathways for community sharing, the results will move your students forward as they notice, reflect on, and appropriate other readers' successful behaviors and problem-solving methods.

Figure 9.1

Ideas for Successful Share Time

1 Invite students to share some things they've noticed during independent reading time (their processes, strategies employed, a shift in their thinking, focusing issues, reading rate, use of a coding system to leave notes in the text, etc.).

2 Ask readers to take a quick survey of favorite lines or passages from their current read and share aloud the one line they really liked.

3 Ask students to write down a book/genre/strategy that was a stretch for them—where they tried out something new. Collect as a quick survey.

4 Give readers opportunities to turn and talk with a partner about something they struggled with today—something that was difficult for them to do.

5 Have students find one word from their reading that they consider to be a "gem" and share it aloud and explain why they chose it.

6 Set aside time for readers to share WOW facts (facts that grab the reader's interest that are not necessarily essential to the text), anecdotes, and/or explanations their group has learned from researching an author or topic of interest.

7 Ask students to share one way they problem solved to restore comprehension when meaning broke down for them.

8 Allow students to take questions from classmates to help resolve an issue in their independent reading.

9 Encourage readers to share their plans for the next workshop. Where are they headed?

10 Partner students to each share one short-term or one long-term goal they have set for themselves as a reader.

Video 9.1 ▶

Reflecting and Goal Setting during Share Time

Children reflect on their reading work and set goals for future work.

Figure 9.2 During share time, children can take the lead. June shares a response to her reading from her notebook and explains her thinking to the class.

Kinds of Shares

Share time is as valuable as your minilesson or independent reading time. Here, you have another opportunity to teach and assess, using different kinds of sessions. Share time can include process, progress, strategy, content shares, and performance. Choosing how to share and who will share is the teacher's role. We always ask students if they would be willing to share beforehand, and then provide support as the student shares, highlighting the work and thinking with the sharer if needed. Let's take a look at five possible sharing formats for this valuable time.

PROCESS SHARE

Process shares are great opportunities for teachers to show students how to think aloud to make their comprehension process visible to other students. After several opportunities to observe their teacher thinking aloud, students can try it on their own, demonstrating aloud how they think through a sentence, passage, or page from their independent reading books. In this way, students can act as mentors for each other, especially if they are sharing their reading processes on a regular basis. While readers share with their peers, teachers can observe firsthand how particular students are using key strategies to make meaning from text. This performance-based assessment allows teachers to see what specific students may need help with. (See *Improving Comprehension with Think-Aloud Strategies* by Jeffrey D. Wilhelmm, 2001).

In addition to being a powerful end-of-workshop reflection, sometimes, process shares come as a mid-workshop interruption, where students share something they'd like to try based on a conversation with a classmate or something they found successful from their small group instruction.

STRATEGY SHARE

The strategy share reinforces the importance of using strategies that are taught. It also shows how individual readers make strategies their own. For example, Taylor is sitting on one of the black cubes next to the chart stand.

He has been asked to share his use of a reading strategy during today's share session. The class comes to the carpet. Brenda gets things started. "Today Taylor showed me how he is using the rereading strategy when he loses his train of thought. Let's listen to how he does this." A strategy share session allows students to showcase their use of a reading strategy to the community. The student-sharer becomes the teacher, highlighting the work they did and how the strategy helped them as a reader. This strategy might be something the student learned during the minilesson, in which case the student will "reteach" something you taught. Or, it could be a strategy the student is using in their own way that you think might also benefit the entire community. Sometimes, a small group will share their successful use of a strategy they've been working on together.

Children love to learn from each other and can often offer a clear explanation to their peers. In a strategy share, readers can highlight what they did and the steps they used (even the steps they invented) to make the strategy useful for their reading. This type of share celebrates students as readers and as agents of their own learning and encourages the community to act strategically as they read.

PROGRESS SHARE

We cannot always stop for a portfolio party or a large celebration to acknowledge the progress we've made as readers during a marking period, but share time is a great way to celebrate on a weekly basis. During progress shares, the student reader celebrates their progress. These shares can include a risk the student took—perhaps trying a new genre, such as Arthurian legends, or a new format, like reading a graphic novel. Students may talk about the progress they've made in developing stamina and endurance—how long they can sustain their reading focus during workshop time. Students can share the progress they've made toward achieving their goals through the work they are doing during the independent reading time of the workshop. They may talk about volume or number of books they've read—in a week or a month in school, at home, or both. Students might even choose to share their volume increase with a line or bar graph that shows their increases by months or seasons. Many

progress shares may stem from one-on-one conferences where you and your students discuss progress toward their goals and how sharing about them can be a way of celebrating their growth while, at the same time, benefiting others in their reading community.

One of our favorite ways for readers to celebrate their progress out loud is through Penny Kittle's (2012) idea of book stacks. Students gather books they've enjoyed and stack the books up, which gives a visual representation of what they've accomplished with their reading. Sharing book stacks is a great way to showcase students' reading identities. Students can choose to create a stack around an author, genre, topic, or theme. For example, they might celebrate the books they've read that have allowed them to see themselves in the pages of the book. As students share book stacks, conversations can generate new stacks. When students talk about favorite authors, genres, and topics, a kind of "stack wisdom" unfolds. The community benefits from learning about the different experiences their peers are having with books. Book stacks are a creative, fun way for students and teachers to share their knowledge of books they want to celebrate and recognize.

Figure 9.3

Remember to model your own readerly life for your students. Here, Brenda shares her book stack with students early in the year and again in the spring and encourages them to build their own book stacks.

Ryan's book stack represents his book choices for the school year and shows how his reading changed over time.

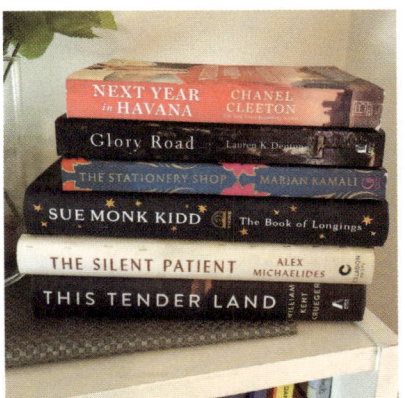

CONTENT SHARE

In a content share, the community gathers to learn about different options for responses by observing and listening to specific content from a fellow community member's response notebook. Students who share explain their responses, showing their work or reading it, and then talking about why they chose to respond in this way. By sharing, they are making their thinking visible to their classmates.

> **TEACHER TIP:** Making a copy of a page from a notebook is a great way to share a student's response. After (or before) they have shared, make a copy, enlarge it, and use it as an anchor chart. Paste the copy of the page on chart paper and have the student add some tips or ways others could also use this response.

Sharing entries from a reader's notebook offers the members of the reading community a glimpse at response possibilities. Content shares may begin with showcasing the work of one student so the others can visualize how to use their reader's notebook or how a specific response could be written. A content share can also highlight how a student uses their notebook in new and unique ways. As the teacher, you can decide if this share will serve as an example of response expectations or show new possibilities.

Figure 9.4 During a content share session, Ethan explains how he has been sketching a comics response format to help him better understand character motivation in his independent reading book.

Content shares can also highlight the work of the whole class at one time. You might consider having children place their notebooks around the room with specific pages open to highlight the way each student approached a particular response option. Other times you might have children choose one response they are proud of and want to share. Children can move around the room to view these responses. Bringing the whole class back together to share what they noticed celebrates the work of the community.

PERFORMANCE SHARES

At times a share session may look and feel like a performance as students read aloud from their independent reading books. Children may choose to read aloud to show how they internally "hear" the voice and inflection of a character. Partners can share what a dialogue may sound like between two characters. Other times, children may read aloud from a selection, portraying its mood by reading with emotion, or showcase their fluency through a reader's theater performance. By asking children to reflect aloud on their oral reading choices, you allow them to showcase the importance of inferring and support their classmates' attempts at this same strategy. Other performances can be in the form of a storytelling theater, complete with props (and even costumes for the primary grades!). These performances work well with fables, fairy tales, and myths. Sometimes, book club members collaborate to write and perform a found poem that captures the essence of their book. Other times, a research group presents their findings in a Google slideshow, a song they composed to a familiar tune, drawings, and captions, or through an infographic. The creative possibilities for performance shares are endless!

Structures and Protocols for Sharing

There are many ways to scaffold or structure share sessions. It's important to keep in mind that not everyone needs to share during a whole class share time. Time constraints and attention spans do not allow for this. However, there are ways to build in share time so that all readers have the opportunity to share their thoughts about the books they are reading. Often, we ask our students to partner up in order to think-pair-share. This can occur at end-of-workshop time, during guided practice directly following teacher modeling in the minilesson, during small group instruction, or in peer reading conferences. Sometimes, we ask students to think-ink-pair-share. This way partners can really listen to each other because they've written the key points they want to share in their journal before they begin to talk. Small group shares can occur during literature circles, book clubs, special interest groups, and collaborative research endeavors. Teacher–student shares regularly occur during reading conferences and can be initiated by the teacher or the student.

Figure 9.5 June prepares to share by noting key points from her notebook responses. She records her thoughts on a notecard that will remind her of what she wants to share with her class.

TEACHER TIP: When you're meeting in a virtual setting, whole group sharing can be complicated and intimidating. In this case, consider taking advantage of your virtual platform's breakout room option to create a more collaborative setting. As the moderator, you can move around to join each room, checking in on the discussion, posting an announcement to all rooms, or even placing a time limit on them.

HUSHED SHARE

During a hushed share, students usually all read the same text/piece of literature or respond to the same prompt. You may have the students write in their notebooks first. Students then randomly volunteer to read their comments aloud. While one student responds, the other students listen attentively. No comments are made, and the sharing continues in a random order until all voices are heard. The teacher can take part and choose to begin the share and/or end it.

THINK-INK-PAIR-SHARE

Think-ink-pair-share is a collaborative strategy that builds in a few minutes for students to consider what they want to share, then write a response before sharing it with a partner, small group, or whole group. This way, there is always 100 percent participation and accountability. Teachers can encourage students to revise their written response after sharing to include new ideas and questions/comments.

QUADRANT RESPONSE

Quadrant response is a great way to do a silent share session in groups of four. Using a sheet of paper folded into quadrants, group members individually respond to their peers' thinking about a rich, complex reflection for sharing. The teacher may suggest lifting a line from a text to write about or analyzing a character's actions or a real-life situation and how it impacts the student's community. Sometimes, students simply write a WOW fact and partners react to it. Each student jots/writes a response or comment in one of the quadrants, then passes their paper, reads what the previous student(s) wrote, and writes their own response to the comments they have read. In this way, a string of silent conversation appears on the paper as the quadrants circle around the table—a collaborative discussion takes place in the form of writing.

FOUR CORNERS

Four corners is a scaffold for sharing that asks students to share their responses to a prompt or question. Each of the four corners of the classroom is labeled with a different response (strongly agree, agree, disagree, strongly disagree). Students move to the corner that best aligns with their thinking. They share their ideas with others in their corner and then come to a consensus that represents their collective opinion. One member of each group shares the result of the discussions with the whole class. This works well to discuss strategy use and check in on how established routines are going.

NUMBERED HEADS TOGETHER

Numbered heads together is a cooperative strategy that holds all students accountable for sharing responses and thinking from their group conversation. Students in a group are numbered (usually three to five students in a group). The teacher poses a question or problem. The group members respond in writing in their reader's notebooks and then share within their group. After the share, groups give a signal (thumbs up) that they are ready to share in whole class. The teacher chooses a number, and students assigned that number stand and share their group's thinking. Another possibility is to allow these chosen students to travel to a new group and share with them. Particularly in reading workshop, numbered heads reinforces the importance of active listening and for students who participate in a group to be able to explain their ideas to others in clear, concise ways. It also gives readers an opportunity to teach or reteach a concept or strategy to a group member who needs some additional help in order to offer a response about the text.

GALLERY WALK

Gallery walk is a discussion technique where readers work together in small groups to collect ideas and respond to various sharing prompts written on pieces of chart paper that are spread across the room. Students circulate in small groups to discuss the question/statement and add their new thinking on the chart paper using a different color marker before moving on to the next chart paper. After rotating all the way through, students return to their first station to read all that was added to their first response. Bring the class back together to discuss what they shared and make final conclusions about what they saw and discussed.

What Is Reading Workshop?

The definition of reading workshop for me has changed over the years. My first take on reading workshop is after the minilesson, the students would read silently while incorporating the strategy that was taught during the group, and the teacher would pull a small group where the students read the same book. As I continued to teach, I educated myself with other learning opportunities and experience in different grade levels and I have somewhat changed my view on reading workshop. Using a mentor text, most likely my read-aloud, I model a strategy or skill that I then ask the students to work on during their independent reading time. Where I used to encourage silent reading, I have now found that this is a valuable time for students to collaborate with their reading partners and still be immersed in the act of reading. The students are eager to share what they just read, a theory they came up with, or a shocking revelation that occurred. They are so excited to read and share that I often can't justify asking them to stop!

Kathleen McLaughlin,
Grade 3 teacher, Franconia Elementary School

Reflection: An Important Aspect of Sharing

One of the most important jobs a teacher has is to encourage students to think about the work they do in a careful, analytical way so they can come to understand what is going well and what is problematic for them. Taking the time to reflect on *what* they've learned and *how* they learned it gives students an opportunity to look back at what they have done, to examine the processes (or strategies) they used, and to think about the importance of their work and growth. We want children to understand

that being reflective means to be curious about our own thinking and to come up with ways to express or name the thinking so others can learn from this. Reflection offers students the chance to slow down, consider the important work they have been doing, and understand that they are the authors of their own learning. This metacognitive process speaks to what Peter Johnston discusses in his book *Choice Words* (2004) as *agency*: "a sense that if they (students) act, and act strategically, they can accomplish their goals" (29).

Building reflection into your share time at the end of reading workshop is a good way to bring closure. Students can reflect and share problem-solving strategies, what they've discovered about themselves as readers, their challenges and successes. Students may be directed by one or two questions a teacher poses before students engage in independent reading. Those questions can reside on an anchor chart or white board to serve as a reminder so students can "get ready" for final reflection. This gathering conversation depends on the collective experiences that children have had during the workshop session.

Video 9.2

The Value of End-of-Workshop Share/Reflection Time

Dr. Aileen Hower talks about the benefits of student's time to share their thinking with others.

Figure 9.6 Third grade students make reading timelines to show their reading growth, reflecting on what they learned from the books and what they learned about themselves as readers.

You might want to have readers reflect periodically in their reader's notebooks, taking the time to write longer entries. The language we use to encourage this kind of reflection sets the tone. Prompting with open-ended questions and sentence stems (see **Figure 9.7**) can be helpful since they are neutral and non-judgmental while pointing the way so the students can do the work. Giving children time to write about their thinking will make their thinking visible. (It is also helpful before we ask them to share verbally, because it means 100 percent of your students are participating and are accountable to engage in metacognition—thinking about their own thinking.) These reflections can be used at individual conferences to help set goals and guide your response to the reader. Thinking about our own thinking is not always a comfortable or natural activity, for our students or for us. It needs to be practiced and modeled. By being intentional about reflecting, we can build a community that is curious and learns together.

Figure 9.7

Questions and Stems for Reflection

- What have you learned about yourself as a reader?
- Can you think of any ways you might improve your use of workshop time?
- What is going to make the biggest difference to you as a reader?
- What do you notice about your reading habits by studying your book log?
- Something I would like others to notice is . . . .
- A question I would like to research is . . . .
- My best moment in reading workshop was . . . .
- An example of when I felt challenged is . . . .
- As I think about our end-of-workshop shares and reflection, one way I could improve my written responses in my notebook is . . . .
- Something I would like to see happen during the workshop is . . . .

Final Thoughts

Sharing and reflection time in a reading workshop offer our readers the opportunity to consider the work they and their classmates have been doing. Our share sessions invite readers to share their thinking orally and in creative written ways, reflecting on their processes, successes, and future goals. Sharing is a practice that promotes caring and respectful learners. It helps students get to know each other and practice both academic and social skills. Sharing gives students opportunities to practice and reinforce speaking, listening, and thinking skills that are crucial to self-reflection, an important habit for students to be able to make sense of and grow from an experience.

In reading workshop, student reflection can lead to deeper reading and using a wider range of reading strategies. It can help readers be better prepared to listen to their peers and engage in thoughtful conversations. Often occurring at the end of the workshop, sharing sessions can help to provide closure for students while giving teachers an opportunity to do some formative assessment as readers share. Reflection helps students set goals and track their progress and can help them reimagine materials, ideas, and texts for future personal use and social benefit. Finally, remember: sharing isn't just for student readers. Reflecting and sharing our thinking with our students helps them see us as people who take time to stop and think about our own reading processes. When we join in on the sharing, students see us as learners, curious and responsive to what we are learning and doing in our community.

Figure 9.8 Students spend the last five minutes of independent reading time using sticky notes to mark new discoveries in their independent reading books as they prepare for their end-of-workshop reflection, a daily routine in their reading workshop.

Stop and Reflect

1. How do you build in time for sharing and reflection during your reading workshop?
2. How can you help your students grow as reflective thinkers? When and how can you best model reflection?

Something to Try

Look over your reading workshop conference notes. What could each child share at some time during the next week? How will they share? Make it a point to encourage and include all your students in your community shares.

Classroom Assessments That Make a Difference

Assessment isn't formative if it doesn't influence learning in a positive way.

— **Peter H. Johnston,**
Choice Words: How Our Language Affects
Children's Learning

In most school systems, a good part of the school year has focused on student assessment. Understanding our purposes for assessment and thinking about how we collect rich data to drive our instruction are important. Assessment should always be purposeful, informative, and useful to us as facilitators of learning. The essential goal of student assessment in the teaching and learning process is to improve student learning. According to Afflerbach (2010), reading assessment tells us a story. It provides a history of our students' accomplishments, and their ability to construct literal, inferential, and critical understandings, as well as a clear understanding of our students' development as readers. Reading assessments allow us to assess the strengths and needs of all our students.

Formative Assessment: Why It Is So Important

According to Peter Johnston (2012), "The heart of formative assessment is finding the edge of students' learning and helping them to take up

responsibilities for growth" (49). We believe these important experiences, including each student's ability to assess their own learning and take note of the learning of their peers, will help all readers move forward. Noticing and appropriating successful practices in conferences, whole-group discussions about literature, share sessions, and reflection time are all part of formative assessment. The National Council of Teachers of English (2013) tells us that "formative assessment is a constantly occurring process, a verb, a series of events in action, not a single tool or a static noun" (3). One of our hardest jobs is to build in time each day for formative assessment practices such as taking some notes as we observe our students as readers. But we cannot stop there. The more difficult part of this process is to also find the time to analyze the data we have gathered and decide what to do with it! As teachers, we strive to improve the ongoing work we do each day with reflective evaluation of that work. The goals of formative assessment are many, but the goals to keep in the foreground of the work we do with children include the following:

- Monitor student learning.
- Use knowledge gleaned from observations, conferences, rubrics, checklists, class discussions, and writing samples to inform instruction (teacher).
- Provide feedback for readers to try new things, set goals, evaluate progress toward goals, build on strengths, and celebrate efforts while becoming more confident and competent.

Reading workshop provides a perfect setting for formative assessment because it is a structured practice designed for student growth and success. Because it takes place over time and provides opportunities for immediate feedback along the way, teacher and student reflection is built into daily routines.

Formative Assessment Practices

In order to make the best use of your time, begin by asking yourself some questions that will help guide your formative assessment practices. What do you really want your students to know and understand? What are they

Video 10.1 ▶

Assessing a Reader

Administering a running record helps a teacher determine readers' strengths and needs.

actually learning and able to recall and use appropriately as strategic readers? What can you do to help your students learn what they need to know in order to move forward as readers (writers, and thinkers)? Then develop tools and methods to collect information to help you answer these questions. Finally, use the information to improve instruction, adapt curricula, and help your students set new goals.

KIDWATCHING

One of the most impactful ways we can establish practices of formative assessment is kidwatching. Yetta Goodman and Gretchen Owocki (2002) widely use this term to describe the intentional ways we track and support student learning. In its basic form, kidwatching is about tuning into kids as they read, write, collaborate, and participate in class. As we do, we collect a series of anecdotes about student development that we can share with families and administrators to provide concrete evidence of the kinds of student learning that traditional testing simply cannot capture.

Of course, it would not be possible to observe every student during the reading workshop every day. Find a way that makes sense to you. For instance, you might identify five students to observe each day and place their names on sticky notes on your clipboard. Keep some extra sticky notes with you in case you want to jot a quick note when you observe a student doing something noteworthy or who is struggling with a concept from your minilesson but may not be on your list for that day. Once you find a method that works for you, make this a daily habit. Remember, student observation can take many forms. Consider the variety of artifacts at your disposal such as exit slips, conference notes, video clips, audio recordings, and anchor charts with students' initials so you can determine who is contributing and who is holding back. As you watch, record the student's name, the date, and the activity you are observing in order to examine these collective notes over a period of time for signs of growth. Kidwatching is important because it is not about tracking just what students *can* do but even more about *how* students make meaning and learn new strategies and skills. By paying attention to how students learn, kidwatching gives teachers information that enables them to differentiate instruction and plan future classroom activities that fit the specific needs of their students. **Figure 10.1** offers some questions to jumpstart your kidwatching observations.

Figure 10.1

Kidwatching Questions

1 What am I observing that helps me describe student engagement during independent reading? Where do they focus their attention?
2 How do students "read" the room when they are responding to a text? Do they move closer to the anchor chart? Are they scanning the word wall to help spell a word for a written response?
3 What do students do when they struggle? How do they problem solve?
4 What strengths are easily observed? Where do students have an area of expertise?
5 What excites students? What are their passions and interests? How do I know?
6 What patterns and preferences can I note?
7 In what ways are students developing as readers? How are they building their reader's identities?
8 What kinds of decisions do readers make during independent reading? Peer conferences? Student–teacher conferences? Small group instruction?
9 What information do students need to know that they don't have?
10 Where do I see the "tracks of my teaching" (evidence that students are using the skills/strategies/procedures examined and demonstrated in my minilessons)?

CONFERENCE NOTES AS ASSESSMENT

Conference notes that show us what children can do as readers provide us with knowledge we can use to plan minilessons, decide on small group composition and instruction, and set individual goals and instructional plans (see **Figure 10.2**). Our notes give us valuable information about our readers and inform our teaching practices with the individual reader and the class. Taking time to write notes while conferring, adding thoughts immediately during and after the conference, and taking time later to reflect on those notes will enable us to plan more effectively for future instruction. When taking notes, consider what the child is showing you through their words and actions.

TEACHER TIP: One of the best ways to get to know the readers in your classroom is through three-book conferences. To start, ask students to bring three books with them to their individual reading conference—a favorite book, a book that has a character they admire and/or identify with, and a book they would change in some way. This type of conference provides valuable information about a student's likes and dislikes and is a wonderful way to get started with initial notes about the readers in your classroom.

Figure 10.2

Taking Notes During Reading Conferences

- Notice strategies the student uses as they describe the work they are doing in their reading.
- Note how the reader approaches the text. Are they excited to talk about the text? Can they hold a conversation about the text? Do they address their feelings and/or make connections with the text? Do they offer an opinion about the text?
- Consider how the reader retells. Are they able to retell with ease? Do they focus on literal details when retelling? Are they making meaning from the text, citing evidence to support their thinking and interpretations?
- Is the reader using strategies you have previously taught?
- What do their body language and tone of voice tell you?

Figure 10.3 As a teacher confers with a student, she records strategies on sticky notes, which she will leave with him as a reminder of what they've worked on.

Regularly reviewing conference notes can help you see growth your readers are making, see evidence of your instruction, assess the reader's ability to use strategies, and make decisions about future work for this student and the community. A reading conference with a child is a chance to listen to the thinking they are doing to make meaning from a text. Keep in mind, simply taking notes doesn't make this formative assessment—it's not until we set aside time to reflect on our observations and, in turn, take action that our notes become true formative assessment.

ADMIT AND EXIT SLIPS

Admit and exit slips are two quick ways to survey the class and gain insight into the understanding of a strategy taught, thinking around a concept that has been introduced or will be introduced, or any work the class is engaged in. These quick formative assessments only take a few minutes to do, gather, and read but can give you valuable information about the readers in your classroom. Admit slips are given before the class comes together. For instance, you might ask questions about the class read-aloud before the day's reading begins as a way to sort out any misconceptions about the concept, setting, or theme. You might ask students to respond on a sticky note that can be shared orally and/or posted on a chart. At times you could have children write a longer thought in their reader's notebooks. In Brenda's class the students were asked to write briefly about the setting in Padma Venkatraman's book *The Bridge Home* before coming to the class read-aloud. Children wrote their thoughts and sketched in their readers' notebooks for a few minutes, and then shared their writing with a partner. As Brenda roved around the room listening in on conversations, she realized the setting was very new to her students and that they would need more background knowledge to fully understand and make meaning of this text. Using an admit slip as a formative assessment allows us to make in-the-moment adjustments to our work.

An exit slip, on the other hand, is used at the end of the workshop and gives students the opportunity to reflect on the work they have been doing during the workshop. You might ask students to respond to a guiding question that refers back to the minilesson that was taught that day or to a class goal. Or, you might ask your children to rate their level of engagement during independent reading time using a number scale on a sticky note and then post them in a line plot graph, giving you a quick glance into how the children view their reading work. You might even consider having children record what worked for them during independent reading time or a strategy they used successfully. Collecting the responses and placing them on a chart as children share their thinking helps everyone reflect on the work of the group while giving you the opportunity to notice trends in thinking and understanding, so you can plan future instruction.

You'll want to note that admit and exit slips are not graded, but they are evaluated. They show us what children can do, and they can help us plan minilessons and, if needed, group students for further instruction. Finally, they offer important opportunities for our own self-reflection, helping us think about "what lessons have stuck, what lessons need to be repeated, what lessons need to be tweaked, and what lessons should be redone from scratch" (Dorfman and Dougherty, 2017, 148).

What Is Reading Workshop?

Our job as teachers in reading workshop should never be to just "cover skills." A true reading workshop experience should foster a love of reading for all students that they will take away with them into their individual homes, future classrooms, and adult lives.

Karen Elizabeth Rhoads,
Grade 4 teacher, Upper Moreland Intermediate School

INDIVIDUAL SURVEYS AND INVENTORIES

In the beginning of the year as we come together as a community of readers, we ask children to complete interest surveys that help us learn about individual reading habits and book choices (see **Chapter 2, Appendix B,** and **Appendix C**). By conferring with students and allowing them to talk with us about their survey, we learn how they view themselves as readers and can help them set goals for the school year or semester.

Moving beyond the first weeks of school and using the surveys throughout the year is a powerful way to use this tool to help readers and teachers notice growth and consider new goals. For example, interest surveys and inventories are a great option for beginning a new unit of study, helping you learn more about your students as nonfiction readers, say, before embarking on a unit that focuses on reading informational text. In this instance, readers could complete an interest survey that includes prompts such as:

- An informational book I have read is . . . .
- A favorite informational book I've read for pleasure is . . . .
- When reading informational books, I like to read about . . . .
- This is how I read an informational book . . . .
- This is what I know about how informational texts are organized . . . .
- When I'm done reading an informational book I want to . . . .
- One thing I'd like to learn about informational reading is . . . . .

Student responses will help you consider what titles they already know, what they need and want to know, and how they feel about this genre. The information can guide you as you differentiate the learning across your next instructional steps.

GOAL SETTING

The ultimate power behind assessments is the way we use them to fine-tune our next instructional goals. As teachers we often set goals for ourselves—personal and professional. Goals to finish teaching a unit by a specific date. Maybe a goal to confer with three students during a workshop period. Or a personal reading goal—spend thirty minutes a night reading for enjoyment during the week. We understand that goals create a vision for where we are going. In the same way, our instructional goals for students and their goals for themselves as readers are critical.

For instance, when Brenda meets with a reader, her conference notes detail her personal goal for that reader based on a variety of assessments. Next to the goal are the steps Brenda will take to help them meet that goal: include them in a small group with the focus on inferring, teach them a specific strategy to use, provide them with a scaffold to use, and so on. This allows Brenda to document the work toward the goal and its success.

Involving children in this process gives them ownership and agency over their learning. When we include the students, we teach them the importance of goal setting and help them create ways to meet their individual goals. June was an avid fiction reader. She devoured books, but after looking over the titles in her book log, she and Brenda realized they were all the same genre. Together they created a goal—read different fiction genres and some nonfiction. They wrote out a plan together and determined who would be responsible. June would ask friends for book suggestions; Brenda would gather some books she thought June would like. June would create a to-read list that included something new as well as her favorite genre, numbering the books to indicate the order she would read them in. After six weeks they would meet together to discuss how the goal was going and what June had learned. When we take advantage of formative assessment in ways that help us and our readers set goals and make plans to meet them, we establish practices that will help them today and as they go forward.

SELF-ASSESSMENT

Providing opportunities across the reading workshop for students to self-reflect can help us better understand them and how they see themselves as readers, writers, and thinkers. Children become more comfortable with reflection and assessment when they realize this work is not meant to "give them a grade" but to help them become stronger readers, writers, and thinkers. Providing children with tools for this type of reflection can ease them into the routine of self-assessment and offers a useful scaffold.

Checklists

There are a variety of checklists you can introduce to help students consider their reading work and progress. Consider what skill, strategy, or procedure you are teaching and then create a checklist. Keeping things simple will make your checklist something children will use and find valuable. A checklist can remind readers of steps they need to take to complete a strategy or task or can help them assess their ability to complete work independently. Having children help you create the checklist often gives students more ownership and increases the likelihood of use. This checklist can be used by teachers and their students with modifications by grade level for student use. For example, **Figure 10.4** shows an example checklist students can use to check in on how they're doing with some typical reading workshop norms.

Figure 10.4

Reading Workshop Survival Skills

☐ Completes classwork assignment in required time

☐ Requests assistance, explanations, or instructions from the teacher when needed

☐ Uses time productively while waiting for teacher assistance or when working independently

☐ Self-advocates—asks thoughtful questions of the teacher when unsure of what to do on schoolwork at appropriate times and in an appropriate manner

☐ Produces quality reader response/notebook entries that connect with the text, class and book club discussions, and conferences

☐ Sets short-term and long-term reading goals

☐ Ignores distractions during independent reading and all class discussions

☐ Is prepared with a book of choice to read and materials and plans for research projects

☐ Knows when to abandon a book and choose a new one

☐ Attends to the speaker with active listening skills in all class discussions, and participates in projects, performances, and team endeavors

Reading Engagement Inventory

A reading engagement inventory is a periodic formative assessment we've found valuable in our reading workshops. We choose to do this once per grading period, but you'll find a time frame that works best for you. Essentially, you set aside a time to simply observe how individual students are engaging in the work of reading and how they are using their workshop time. When we observe our students, we use a code to make record-keeping easy (see **Figure 10.5**). It is important to find a coding system that is simple and comfortable for you to use. During independent reading, we stroll around the room, taking a good look to see if students are: engaged in reading (**+**); engaged most of the time (**✓**); responding in writing to the text (**r**); searching for a good book in the classroom library (**❙**) (note how long it takes a student to select a book or if they are using the library to avoid reading); working at a computer or on a device to research/read online (**○**); or distracted (**d**) (make a note to indicate trips to the bathroom, supply center, water fountain or pencil sharpener; pretending to read by flipping pages; abandoning a book too quickly; gazing out the window; watching the teachers or other adults in the room).

To implement engagement inventories on your own, you might select four different students to observe on any given day, record the code in the row next to the student's name every five minutes for fifteen minutes, then look over your data to plan for individualized instruction and goal setting. Depending on the grade level you are working with and your students' maturity level, you may want to share the results in one-on-one conferences in order to help readers set goals for themselves. The information can be shared during parent conferences, too, to talk about each student's reading behaviors.

Figure 10.5

Coding Reading Engagement Inventories

+ = engaged

✓ = somewhat engaged

r = responding in writing

p = partner reading

○ = reading/researching online

❙ = library

d = distracted

Write Me a Letter

Beginning in third grade, we can ask students to write us a letter to tell us about concerns, questions, and ideas they would like to share with us about their reading goals and progress. Some teachers like to create a "mailbox" where students can place their letters. Envelopes and choice of stationery help to make this self-reflection a more personal experience. These letters are treasures, and we love responding to them! If you're having difficulty finding the time to respond to each student, perhaps limit mailbox access to once a week or designate one or two marking periods for this activity. The value behind this formative assessment is that, because it's such a private correspondence, you are likely to learn a lot more about your student's reading anxieties, challenges, celebrations, and thoughts about how to make reading workshop even more successful.

Final Thoughts

Assessment is an important part of daily practice, giving us myriad opportunities to revise our instruction and provide immediate, ongoing feedback for our students. Practical assessments give teachers the knowledge they need to help students grow and evolve into mature, confident readers. Assessment practices that include opportunities for us to reflect on our teaching and give students opportunities to reflect on their learning will provide rewarding outcomes. By valuing readers as a group of individual and diverse learners, we can provide them with authentic assessment experiences in reading workshop.

Stop and Reflect

1. How do you use formative assessment practices during your reading workshop/reading classroom sessions?
2. In what ways do you keep records of daily observations of performance, readerly behavior, and student progress? What are you learning from these observations?

Something to Try

Make a list of the ways you currently evaluate your students' reading abilities and readerly behaviors. Now, look at your list. What do you want to eliminate? What would you like to add to your list? Share your list with a colleague, perhaps a grade level partner. Talk about how your list represents what you value most for your students as readers.

Afterword

Let's Get Started

As you close this book and reflect on the discussions we've had along the way, you may be wondering what to do first. How do you get started building a thriving reading workshop and community? We trust those first steps will come to you—and, as always, we have suggestions!

First, don't feel that you have to begin this journey alone. Find a mentor. One thing that continually motivates us is the group of colleagues that surround us with their support and encouragement. Mentors are those people you can go to when you want questions answered, when you need a suggestion for a book, or when you need to honestly share your frustrations and successes. You can trust a mentor. A mentor builds your energy toward the work you are doing. Consider a colleague who has experience with reading workshop. Or a teacher who is passionate about their work and is willing to learn with you. Maybe you'll find a mentor through Twitter. Or maybe a mentor will find you. In *Thrive: Five Ways to (Re)Invigorate Your Teaching* (2014), Meenoo Rami offers numerous suggestions for finding a mentor and working with them. She reminds us that mentors can be formal or casual, and you can have more than one.

Getting support doesn't have to be confined to the school building where you teach. Consider ways to build and connect with a larger professional learning network. The International Literacy Association (ILA) and its state and local organizations have been an inspiration and a place for personal and educational growth for both of us. It has been through our work with these organizations that we have tried new ideas and pursued inquiry projects, receiving the support of a network of educators that includes K–12 and beyond from many schools, private and public. Other communities to consider include the National Council of Teachers of English (NCTE) and its local and state organizations as well as other educator groups like a chapter of Alpha Delta Kappa, an international honorary society for women educators.

You'll find lots of supportive mentors and communities online as well. Find educators to follow on Twitter and participate in chats. Read blogs such as the Stenhouse blog or blogs written by teachers and authors of books we've showcased here. Listen to podcasts and sign up for webinars and conferences. Consider TED-Ed lessons on video and TED Talks from inspiring teachers as well as Edutopia. There are many amazing avenues of support out there; you are not alone.

Another way to get started with reading workshop is to live a readerly life that can serve as a model to the children you work with. The greatest tool we can use is our own experiences. When we use mentor texts and share our own thinking about something we've noticed or how we've used a certain strategy to make the meaning clear, it helps students to grasp concepts more thoroughly. When we model our own reading decision-making through think-alouds, we make the reading process visible to our students, helping our young readers make a greater connection to the text. Likewise, when you create and use your own reading journal, it becomes a great tool to use during conferences and small group instruction. You can showcase your journaling efforts during end-of-workshop final reflection or even during minilessons as a model to share with the class. By crafting, utilizing, and sharing your own reading journal, you can create a resource directly connected to the important reading workshop concepts and routines you hope your students will learn.

Finally, an important part of living a readerly life is to simply make time to read. Students need to see us as readers. By reading regularly and responding in a reading journal, you can better understand and model the thinking you hope to see students use and establish yourself as a bona fide member of their reading community. Reading grade level texts will also give you a wealth of ideas and books to suggest to students. Reading for your own pleasure and growth will give you readerly experiences you can share with your students.

As you take these initial steps forward, we are here for you, and we'd love to hear from you. Keep us posted with your questions, successes, and challenges via social media, using the hashtag #WelcomeRW to join our ongoing conversation. Congratulations on beginning what we know will be one of the most rewarding journeys of your professional career—one full of books, reading, reflection, conversation, growth, and—most of all—joy!

Brenda   Lynne

Appendices

Appendix A   Book Recommendations to Help Build and Celebrate a Reading Workshop Community

- *How to Read a Story* by Kate Messner. 2015. Chronicle Books. The author helps readers celebrate the joy found in sharing a picture book with someone through reading it aloud.
- *The Day You Begin* by Jacqueline Woodson. 2012. Nancy Paulsen Books. This refreshing, nonlinear story is about Angelina as she begins the school year and the class is asked to share out about their summer travels. Text and illustrations effectively work together to convey her feelings as she reflects on her own summer spent at home and finally finds her place in her new classroom.
- *I Walk with Vanessa: A Story about a Simple Act of Kindness* by Kerascoet. 2018. Schwartz & Wade. One girl's upstanding action inspires her schoolmates to join and support a bullied child in this wordless, important story.
- *All Are Welcome* by Alexandra Penfold. 2018. Knopf Books for Young Readers. The author and illustrator celebrate a school community as a common ground where families of all kinds connect and share in their children's educational journey.
- *Alma and How She Got Her Name* by Juana Martinez-Neal. 2018. Candlewick. Alma Sofia Esperanza José Pura Candela thinks her name is too long, so her father tells her the story of where it came from.
- *Green Green: A Community Gardening Story* by Marie Lamba and Baldev Lamba. 2017. Farrar, Straus, & Giroux. This story is based on an idea of working together to clean up and beautify the neighborhood. It inspires people of all ages and races to make a difference in the world we live in.
- *Just Ask! Be Different, Be Brave, Be You* by Sonia Sotomayor. 2019. Philomel Books. The author explores the differences that make each of us unique. Written in the voices of children, including Sotomayor and the illustrator, Rafael Lopez, a beautiful garden is created as questions are asked and answered.
- *Outside, Inside* by LeUyen Pham. 2021. Roaring Brook Press. A poignant response to the Covid 19 pandemic that honors essential workers and celebrates how communities came together to face challenges in recent times.
- *Hip Hop Speaks to Children: A Celebration of Poetry with a Beat* by Nikki Giovanni (ed). 2008. Sourcebook Inc. Poets range from Langston Hughes to Queen Latifah. Appealing to audiences of any age, from pre-K kids to great-grandparents, these vibrant chants will build community as students engage with material not found together elsewhere.
- *Be You!* by Peter Reynolds. 2020. Orchard Books. All children are unique and special. The author reminds us to celebrate our special qualities.
- *I Am Enough* by Grace Byers. 2018. Balzar + Bray. A beautiful picture book about loving who you are, respecting others, and being kind to one another with a reminder that we are free to follow our hearts and be ourselves.
- *Poems Aloud* by Joseph Coelho. 2020. Wide Eyed Editions. This collection of poems offers a fun way to start each morning with a choral read and a performance—a great way to gather children together and build common experiences.

- *My Bother Charlie* by Holly Robinson Peete and Ryan Elizabeth Peete. 2010. Scholastic Press. Told from a sister's point of view, this picture book helps raise awareness and understanding of autism. This book offers a great way into discussions about togetherness, hope, and love.

- *Sumi's First Day of School Ever* by Joung Un Kim and Soyung Pak. 2003. Viking Books for Young Readers. The first day of school can be scary and lonely when you do not know the language. This is a thoughtful picture book about a young Korean girl on her first day of school.

- *A Friend Like You* by Frank Murphy and Charnaie Gordon. 2021. Sleeping Bear Press. This book celebrates the many ways children can be friends. It encourages children to be curious, forgiving, accepting, and kind friends.

- *Wishtree* by Katherine Applegate. 2017. Feiwel & Friends. This chapter book is told by the oak tree, Red, who tells the story of a neighborhood coming together to fight bigotry and save a tree that holds the wishes of the community.

- *Your Name Is a Song* by Jamilah Thompkins-Bigelow. 2020. The Innovation Press. This book celebrates the beauty, history, and magic behind names. Pronunciations are included throughout the book so that students and teachers can pronounce the names and hear their rhythm and beat.

- *Black Is a Rainbow Color* by Angela Joy. 2020. Roaring Brook Press. In this book's author's note, Joy states that "Black is not just a color but a culture, too." Her intention is to share all that is beautiful, loving, and strong about a culture, history, and celebration of African Americans to help create safe and welcoming spaces for all children.

- *What Is a Refugee?* by Elise Gravel. 2019. Schwartz & Wade. A simple book to introduce students to the meaning of the term "refugee." Humanizing and compassionate, the book ends with a two-page spread with quotes from refugees and another two-page spread with short bios about famous refugees.

- *Ada's Violin: The Story of the Recycled Orchestra of Paraguay* by Susan Hood. 2016. Simon & Schuster Books for Young Readers. The true story of Ada Ríos growing up in a community of people who live and feed themselves by picking through the tons of trash generated by the capital city of Paraguay, and salvaging items to recycle and sell. When music teacher Favio Chávez arrives, he discovers there are not enough instruments to go around. The children create them out of material from the discarded trash and travel around the world to perform.

- *Drawn Together* by Minh Le. 2018. Little, Brown Books for Young Readers. Much of this timeless story is told through the stunning illustrations of Dan Santat. A young boy and his Vietnamese grandfather do not share a common language, but their shared love of drawing connects them and brings them closer.

- *Going Down Home with Daddy* by Kelly Starling Lyons. 2019. Peachtree Publishing Company. Lil Alan tries to find the perfect gift to give his great-grandma for their annual family reunion. Lyon explores the power and importance of rich family traditions and the connections we have to a special place that binds us together.

- *Fry Bread: A Native American Family Story* by Kevin Noble Maillard. 2019. Roaring Brook Press/Macmillan. This multi-award-winning book depicts a modern Native American family through a traditional food: fry bread. This book celebrates the history, memory, and community of Native American people.

- *Mango, Abuela, and Me* by Meg Medina. 2017. Candlewick. When Mia's abuela comes to live with them, Mia and her grandmother cannot speak to each other because they speak two different languages. Readers watch their relationship blossom and grow as the pair navigate the language and cultural barriers between them.

- *Crown: An Ode to a Fresh Cut* by Derrick Barnes. 2017. Bolden Books. A trip to the barbershop by a young African-American boy is told through the boy's eyes. See the barbershop and dream with the boy as he imagines who he can become after his "fresh cut."

- *Meet Yasmin* by Saadia Faruqi. 2018. Picture Window Books, a Capstone Book (series—Early Reader Chapter Books). Yasmin is a Pakistani American girl with great energy who solves many fears and problems children face. The books in this series are perfect for young readers who will enjoy Yasmin's second-grade antics.

- *Jasmine Toguchi* (series) by Debbi Michiko Florence. 2015. Farrar, Straus and Giroux. Jasmine, an eight-year-old Japanese American girl, is the heroine of this series. Each book takes readers into Jasmine's family and traditions as she learns life lessons applicable to all students. (Grades 1–3)

- *Merci Suárez Changes Gears* by Meg Medina. 2018. Candlewick Publishers. Winner of the 2019 Newbery Award, this book tells the story of sixth grader Merci Suarez as she navigates sixth grade as a "scholarship" student at a private school in Florida. Merci deals with school and friendship issues as well as problems that arise in her Cuban American household when her grandfather becomes ill. (Middle Grades)

- *The Bridge to Home* by Padma Venkatraman. 2019. Puffin Books. On the streets of Chennai, India, two runaway sisters discover friendship and family with two homeless boys when they find shelter on an abandoned bridge. As they scavenge for food and to make a living, they learn about freedom and independence, loyalty, and taking care of each other. (Middle grade chapter book)

- *Save Me a Seat* by Sarah Weeks and Gita Varadarajan. 2016. Scholastic Press. Joe and Ravi are two boys who are from two different backgrounds, American and Indian. As school starts they find themselves with common problems—finding friends and dealing with a bully. Over the course of the novel they learn about friendship, fitting in, family, and cultural differences. (Grades 3–7)

Appendix B Four Square Interest Survey, Grades 3–6

Note to Teachers: This survey is intended to be given to students at various times throughout the year to note how reading interests have changed. Each square can be dated for reference and placed in the student's reading folder or portfolio to document reading growth and change.

What different kinds of reading do you enjoy?	
I am interested in . . . One experience I had was . . . I remember this reading/project because . . . Does the reading you enjoy most connect with something else you enjoyed doing or will do again? Date:	I am interested in . . . One experience I had was . . . I remember this reading/project because . . . Does the reading you enjoy most connect with something else you enjoyed doing or will do again? Date:
I am interested in . . . One experience I had was . . . I remember this reading/project because . . . Does the reading you enjoy most connect with something else you enjoyed doing or will do again? Date:	I am interested in . . . One experience I had was . . . I remember this reading/project because . . . Does the reading you enjoy most connect with something else you enjoyed doing or will do again? Date:

©2023 Brenda Krupp and Lynne Dorfman. From *Welcome to Reading Workshop* (Portsmouth, NH: Stenhouse). May be photocopied for classroom use only.

Draw, label, and/or write a sentence to respond to each prompt.

My favorite books are . . .	I like to read about . . .
My reading spot is . . .	**Books I hope to read this year . . .**

©2023 Brenda Krupp and Lynne Dorfman. From *Welcome to Reading Workshop* (Portsmouth, NH: Stenhouse). May be photocopied for classroom use only.

Minilesson: _____

Type	
Focus	
Mentor Text	
Teacher Notes	
Hook	
Explicit Teaching (Purpose/Model/Explain)	
Application (Guided and Independent Practice)	
Closure	
(Independent Reading, Small Groups, Book Clubs)	
Sharing/ Reflection	

©2023 Brenda Krupp and Lynne Dorfman. From *Welcome to Reading Workshop* (Portsmouth, NH: Stenhouse). May be photocopied for classroom use only.

Appendix D

Minilesson:	**Choosing a Book for Independent Reading**
Type	Procedural Minilesson
Focus	How to Choose a Book
Mentor Text	Teacher's Personal Reading Stack
Teacher Notes	Students love choice, but with so many books to choose from choice can become overwhelming. Some want to read *the* "chapter" book everyone wants. Others are clamoring for the book with a cute puppy on the cover, or the longest book they can find. And some just choose the first book they find because they aren't sure how to make an informed decision. This is a lesson that aims to help readers intentionally select books and reflect on the choices they're making. This conversation could be held early in the school year, explored over numerous days, or returned to periodically to review procedures.
Hook	Bring some of your shoes to class. These should be different types of shoes and comfort levels. (Example: slippers or flip flops or worn shoes, sneakers, comfortable but not-for-play shoes, high heels or dress shoes with little comfort, boots). Gather books that you are reading or have on your "to be read" stack. These books should reflect different reading purposes and difficulties so you can illustrate how readers choose books for many different purposes.

Explicit Teaching (Purpose/Model/ Explain)	**Purpose:** *Readers, today I want to talk to you about selecting books, which can be difficult when there are so many choices. I've noticed that some of you are choosing books because you like the cover or your friend is reading the same book. I want to teach you that choosing a book is personal and important if you want to grow as a reader.* **Model:** Place a selection of your shoes and books in front of the class. *Each shoe "fits" me and is worn for a specific purpose, just as each book "fits" but is read for a different purpose.* As you describe each shoe and its purpose, model the shoe and walk around in it. Children will quickly see that while you can walk in "spike heels", you would never wear them to play a game on the playground. Connect the analogy as you highlight a book from your stack that requires a lot of work, feels great to start out but can quickly become uncomfortable. Continue making the connection from various shoes and purposes for reading books, creating an anchor chart, comparing your shoes with reading habits. You can illustrate the chart with photographs of the shoes later.

• **Too Easy** (slippers, flip flops) – I know all the words. – I get bored. – NO work.	• **Easy** (sneakers) – I read with confidence. – I get it! – I can retell easily. – I know the words.	• **On My Own** (shoes for comfort) – I know what the words mean. – I read smoothly and with expression. – I use strategies well.	• **Challenging** (dress shoes) – I can figure it out. – I must take my time and use strategies AND I want to.	• **Not yet** (too big) – Words are hard. – I'm choppy, frustrated, confused. – My strategies aren't working as well.

Application (Guided and Independent Practice)	**Guided Practice:** Readers create notebook pages in their reader's notebooks using the headers from the anchor chart. They move to the library and begin to create lists of books they have read or want to read under each heading. As you circulate, note who can easily record books in each category and who is struggling. This is an opportunity to get to know your readers and their choices. Talking with them about why they placed a book in the different categories will help you offer new book suggestions.
Closure	Remind readers that periodically returning to these lists allows them to notice how they develop as readers. They can see their interests change as well as their abilities, check off books they have read, or move books to different categories as they realize the reading growth they have made. Adding books to these lists keeps the book source alive.

(Independent Reading, Small Groups, Book Clubs)	
Sharing/ Reflection	After independent reading time, students share out how they used their lists to help them choose books for themselves and create lists of books they will try later.

Minilesson:	**Ways to Code Nonfiction**

Type	Response Minilesson
Focus	Coding nonfiction text to recall information
Mentor Text	*Animals Nobody Loves* by Seymour Simon
Teacher Notes	This is an inquiry lesson that invites readers to create a system to code text so that the information is easy to access when citing text in a written response and in conversation.
Hook	Bring *Animals Nobody Loves* to the lesson. This book follows a pattern of introducing a photograph of an animal that is not well-loved by most people, as the author challenges this with informational text about what makes the animal, in fact, worthy of our awe. *"Readers, we have been reading this book* (hold up book) *and have been discovering many interesting facts about some animals that are not well liked by people.* (Show photographs of animals from pages you have already read to the class. This is sure to illicit responses about what they remember and find unusual or disgusting.) *There sure was a lot of information in these paragraphs and I'm wondering how we can remember and organize the information so we can use it to respond to questions."*
Explicit Teaching (Purpose/Model/Explain)	**Purpose:** Invite readers to share similar ideas, then continue the conversation with an inquiry. *"With so many different ideas in the text, how can we quickly locate information to support our thoughts without rereading the entire text? Are there ways we could use a sticky note to help us categorize the facts? Do you do anything to help you recall specific parts of a book? Let's work with our reading partners to come up with some ways to use a code and these sticky notes to mark the text so we can recall information."*
Application (Guided and Independent Practice)	**Guided Practice:** At this point children separate into smaller groups to brainstorm and record ideas in their notebooks. Move from group to group offering encouragement, asking for clarification, and, perhaps, spending more time with groups that struggle. It is a good idea to have the book open on a document reader to a page you have already read to the class, so students will be able to consider the information as they decide on ways to code the text. *"Readers, let's regroup and see what you have come up with."* Children regather on the carpet in front of the chart stand where the anchor chart is prepared with a title. Ask groups to choose their best strategy to share and collect as many ideas as time allows, leaving others to be added to the chart later. Children offer their ideas and explain how to use the strategy, which may include: Ways to Code Informational Text • Put a check mark on a sticky note for information that supports the author's main idea. • Put an exclamation mark on a sticky note to mark information that is something you find interesting and want to share with the class. • Put question mark on a sticky note where you are confused and need clarification. (These are just a few ways to code text, and the chart can be modified and changed for different types of nonfiction text.) *Let's try these codes with this page of the text.* Place an uncoded page under a document camera and read the page together. Give reading partners an opportunity to talk together about where they might mark the text. Then reread the text and have children suggest where to place stickies and why.
Closure	Remind students of the work they did and why this is an important strategy. *Readers, today we created a coding system to help us locate specific information in the text. This will help us when we are reading longer text and when we need to support our ideas with specific examples.* At this point you may want to give students a short nonfiction text so they can try the strategy independently, or they can use a nonfiction book from their self-selected stack. Then send them off to read independently.
(Independent Reading, Small Groups, Book Clubs)	
Sharing/Reflection	At the close of the workshop, have a student or two share their use of the coding system and explain how it helped them.

	Minilesson: _____	**Theme with *Jabari Jumps***

Type	Skill/Strategy Minilesson
Focus	Identifying the Theme (Grade 3 or above)
Mentor Text	*Jabari Jumps* by Gaia Cornwall
Teacher Notes	It's tempting to jump into identifying and analyzing the theme too early after reading a text. That should be reserved for a later date when students have a solid grasp on the text they are reading as well as on the meaning of "theme." Before you ask students, "What is the theme?" they first need to have a solid grasp of the literal meaning of the text (plot, setting, characters, conflict, etc.). Identifying and analyzing theme is a skill that requires explicit teaching and practice. To that end, this lesson should grow from a second or third rereading of a mentor text you've already been using with your students. In this lesson we revisit *Jabari Jumps*, a class favorite.
Hook	Invite students to turn and talk with partners about *Jabari Jumps* as they look over the cover. Remind students that Jabari has passed his swimming test and is ready to jump from the diving board. Direct students to listen for ways the author reveals Jabari's feelings throughout the story and how his feelings change. Most kids have faced some kind of challenge at home or in school; Jabari changes as he faces a challenge at the swimming pool.
Explicit Teaching (Purpose/Model/ Explain)	*"Readers, today we are going to look at how a main character changes and grows to determine the theme of the story. The theme is a significant statement that the story is making about life. It is what the story teaches readers. Theme focuses on the deeper meaning or message that the reader is meant to consider, a statement that people can apply to their own lives or world in some way."* Note that a one-word topic cannot label a theme. For example, someone might say the theme of a text is freedom, power, family, love, friendship. These words are topics that are important to the text, but it does not become a theme until a statement is made about the topic.
	Model: Create a timeline of Jabari's actions and think aloud to describe how he was feeling. For example, on the second page Jabari announces to his dad that he is ready to jump off the diving board. The illustrator shows Jabari smiling. Later, we read, "I think tomorrow might be a better day for jumping," showing that he now is feeling unsure and a little scared. As you plot the timeline and think about the feelings connected with the actions, students can start to think about what message they have discovered in the author's words.
	Suggest a possible a theme and write it on the board or chart paper: *It takes some courage to move outside your comfort zone and try something new.* Explain to students that your theme has to do with the topic–courage–and that your statement of theme is a full sentence. The idea can apply to almost everyone, not just to Jabari. You might also suggest this theme: *Sometimes you need the support of a trusted other in order to meet a new challenge.* Providing two statements of theme illustrates that there can be multiple options when identifying theme. Interpretation is based on readers' prior experiences and knowledge. If their thematic statement can be supported by evidence, it is correct!
Application (Guided and Independent Practice)	**Guided Practice:** Students work as partners or in triads to read a fable and try to come up with one or several theme statements. Ask students to write their theme statements in their reading response journals, and remind them that theme statements are written as sentences. The following questions can help students get started: **1.** What does the author think about this topic? **2.** What message do you think the author wants you to consider about this topic? **3.** How do you connect personally to the theme of the story? **4.** How does the theme of the story relate to the world or to humanity in general? **5.** Does the theme of this story remind you of the theme of something else you have read/watched?
Closure	Groups share these themes as you record them on an anchor chart. As they share out, examine each group's statement of theme for its universal appeal. Can we apply it to our own lives? As you send readers off for independent reading, remind them to be thinking about the theme of the texts they choose to spend their time reading.
(Independent Reading, Small Groups, Book Clubs)	
Sharing/ Reflection	Close your workshop by inviting students to reflect on and share out responses to the following questions: • What have you discovered about theme? How would you describe it to someone else? • How is the theme different from the topic? • What strategies did you use to help you come up with a theme statement?

Appendix E Classroom Library Thinking/ Talking Points

Yes	No	Statements
		1. There are a minimum of 15–20 books per student.
		2. I purge my library from time to time weeding out old, tattered, or worn books so the library books are attractive, up-to-date, and in good condition.
		3. My library materials reflect the range of levels in my classroom.
		4. The students in my classroom can find books that are appropriate for their independent reading level, as well as increasing levels of text complexity.
		5. My library contains a variety of materials: books, magazines, eBooks, catalogs, etc.
		6. At least half of my library contains informational texts.
		7. My library has a wide array of genres: picture books, chapter books, poetry, folktales, fairy tales, joke books, historical fiction, mysteries, series, classics, biographies, etc. and topics.
		8. I have multiple copies of popular books.
		9. My books (30%) are new, published in the last 5–10 years.
		10. The library books reflect cultural diversity.
		11. I consider student suggestions when adding books to my library.
		12. The library is accessible to all students.
		13. The books are organized and arranged in a logical and clear manner.
		14. My students understand how the books are arranged.
		15. My students often help with the classroom library's organization.
		16. The organization and labels invite browsing and help students find materials easily.
		17. Most of my books are arranged with the covers facing out.
		18. I have a display area to highlight books and promote reading.
		19. Children use the library throughout the day.
		20. My library is inviting. It makes children want to choose books and read.

©2023 Brenda Krupp and Lynne Dorfman. From *Welcome to Reading Workshop* (Portsmouth, NH: Stenhouse). May be photocopied for classroom use only.

Appendix F Areas to Explore During a Reading Conference

- Listen to the student read aloud to determine fluency.

- Discuss the setting, a character, a significant event, or the problem in the story.

- Ask a question to get the child to think more deeply about the text.

- Ask the student if there's a part that was confusing or difficult to understand.

- Review the student's list of books read or reading interests. Together, set a new reading goal.

- Discuss written responses in the student's reader response journal.

- Ask some questions to assess the student's present attitude toward reading. Has it changed in some way? What caused the change?

- Jumpstart a discussion with a response starter such as:

    - I began to think of . . .
    - I wonder why . . .
    - I know the feeling . . .
    - I noticed . . .
    - I love the way . . .
    - I was surprised . . .
    - I really can't understand . . .
    - I thought . . .
    - If I had been . . .
    - I never thought about . . .
    - What if . . .
    - I think the author . . .
    - It reminds me of . . .
    - I can't believe . . .
    - I wonder what would happen if . . .

Appendix G   Protocols for Book Club and Small Group Discussion

The following protocols can be introduced throughout the year and used to keep students talking in a small group format, including student-led book clubs. By varying the protocols for discussion, you can help your students take turns, encourage response from everyone, and keep everyone interested and engaged. In time, you'll see children begin to use these protocols independently as they form book clubs or discuss books with their peers.

Think-Pair-Share

This practice gives confidence to students who might not share their thinking in a larger group and involves a three-step cooperative structure. First, students think silently about a question posed by the teacher or discussion leader. Individuals then pair up during the second step and exchange thoughts. In the third step, the pairs share their responses with other pairs or the entire group. It is usually a good idea to have the individuals that are sharing with the whole group (or the entire book club) explain what their partner said in order to promote good listening skills.

Merry Go Round

Each student takes a very quick turn sharing with the team a thought or reaction to a prompt posed by the teacher or a member of the book club. Responses should be quick one-to-five-word phrases in order to keep the session moving quickly and keep thoughts concise.

Put Your Two Cents In

Each student has two tokens to use as talking pieces. In groups of four, each student takes a turn by putting one token in the center of the table and sharing their idea. Once everyone has shared once, each student then puts one more token in at a time and responds to what someone else in the group has shared, for example, "I agree with _____ because . . ." or "I don't agree with _____ because . . . ."

Stop and Say Something

To prepare for book club meetings, each person individually reads a portion of the text up to where the group has decided to stop. The group members "stop and say something" pre-determined by the book club members (Beers 2002). When everyone has reached the stopping point, the group members "stop and say something" (Beers 2002) about what they read. This might be anything from a prediction about what will happen next to a question or opinion to a sentence or phrase and its significance. Readers might evaluate a character's behavior or offer a personal connection or a connection with another text, film, or article. This protocol is a great way to help readers monitor their comprehension, especially when it is breaking down (if you have nothing to say about what you have read!).

Appendix G   Protocols for Book Club and Small Group Discussion

Save the Last Word

Readers read a selection of texts and choose two to three quotes that particularly caught their attention. (Option—students write the quote on one side of a card and why they chose it on the other side.) The first reader reads his/her quote aloud without commenting on it (that comes later!). Next, each person has one minute to comment on the quote (If they agree . . . disagree . . . with the quote, or if it makes them think of something related). Then, the reader who initially presented the quote has two minutes to respond to everyone's comments and share out why they selected the quote—this is the last word! Finally, you can repeat the process for each group member. (Adapted from *Creating Classrooms for Authors and Inquirers*, 2nd edition, by Kathy G. Short and Jerome C. Harste, with Carolyn Burke (Portsmouth, NH: Heinemann, 1996.)

Fishbowl

The fishbowl protocol allows the class to observe a book club in action. Children can watch for successful conversation starters as well as ways to respond to each other. The fishbowl is a peer-learning strategy in which some participants are in an outer circle observing a group in the center. In this protocol, both those in the inner and those in the outer circles have roles to fulfill. Those in the center model a particular practice or strategy. The outer circle acts as observers with the goal of learning from the interactions of the center group. Fishbowls can be used to assess things like comprehension or group work behaviors or as a model for reading strategies and discussion techniques. Afterward, allow time for inner circle members share how it felt to be inside and outer circle members to respectfully share their observations and insights. Discuss how the fishbowl could improve all group interactions and conversations. (You could use this information to create an anchor chart for future reference.)

Appendix H Questions for a Reading Conference

This list was created as a guide to help you conduct successful conferences. Note that it is not exhaustive or prescriptive. We encourage you to pick and choose which questions will best move each student forward as a developing reader and to consider collaborating with colleagues to revise this list to fit your students' unique needs.

Monitoring for Understanding and Reading Identity

- Were there any confusing parts?
- What can you do when you're confused?
- Is this book "just right" for you? Why or why not?
- Assess your reading list. Is it robust or limited? How so?

Becoming a Critical Thinker

- Would you recommend this book to other students?
- Will you decide to keep reading or to abandon this book? Why?
- What life lessons are offered?
- Would you like to have these characters in your actual life? Explain.
- How does this book compare with this author's other books?

Extending Reading Selections

- Have you read [title of book] by [name of author]? I think you would like it because . . . (name the genre and connect with an interest the student has or a book they have read that is similar).
- What are you thinking about reading next?
- Can I interest you in trying a new author/genre? I have some of my favorites here in this bin. Shall we look at them?

Examining Problem-Solving Strategies

- That word is difficult to sound out. Let me show you a way to figure out that word with context clues. (Or—Wow, that was a hard word. How did you figure the word out?)
- In today's mini-lesson, we learned about. . . . Have you tried that strategy?
- Have you used a strategy to help you solve a reading problem today? What did you do? Did it work?
- What problems have you had that I can help you with?

References

Afflerbach, Peter (ed.). 2010. "Introduction." In *Essential Readings on Assessment*. Newark, DE: International Reading Association, 1.

Afflerbach, Peter, P. David Pearson, and Scott G. Paris. 2008. "Clarifying Differences between Reading Skills and Reading Strategies." *The Reading Teacher* 6, no. 5, 364–373.

Allington, Richard. 2002. "What I've Learned about Effective Reading Instruction: From a Decade of Studying Exemplary Elementary Classroom Teachers." *Phi Delta Kappan* June: 742.

Allington, Richard L., Kimberly McCuiston, and Monica Billen. 2015. "What Research Says about Text Complexity and Learning to Read." *The Reading Teacher* 68, no. 7: 491–501. https://doi.org/10.1002/trtr.1280.

Allyn, Pam, and Ernest Morrell. 2016. *Every Child a Super Reader: 7 Strengths to Open a World of Possible*. New York: Scholastic.

Atwell, Nancie. 2007. *The Reading Zone: How to Help Kids Become Skilled, Passionate, Habitual, Critical Readers*. New York: Scholastic.

Atwell, Nancie, and Anne Atwell Merkel. 2016. *The Reading Zone: How to Help Kids Become Skilled, Passionate, Habitual, Critical Readers*. 2nd ed. New York: Scholastic.

Barnhouse, Dorothy, and Vicki Vinton. 2012. *What Readers Really Do: Teaching the Process of Meaning Making*. Portsmouth, NH: Heinemann.

Bishop, Rudine Sims. 1990. "Mirrors, Windows, Sliding Glass Doors." *Perspectives: Choosing and Using Books for the Classroom* 6, no. 3 (Summer).

Boushey, Gail, and Joan Moser. 2019. *The CAFE Book: Engaging All Students in Daily Literacy Assessment*. 2nd ed. Portland, ME: Stenhouse.

Buckner, Aimee. 2009. *Notebook Connections: Strategies for the Reader's Notebook*. Portland, ME: Stenhouse.

Burkins, Jan, and Kari Yates. 2021. *Shifting the Balance: Six Ways to Bring the Science of Reading into the Balanced Literacy Classroom*. Portsmouth, NH: Stenhouse.

References

Calkins, Lucy. 2001. *The Art of Teaching Reading*. New York: Addison-Wesley Educational Publishers.

Cherry-Paul, Sonja, Colleen Cruz, and Mary Ehrenworth. 2020. "Making Reading Workshop Work." *Educational Leadership* 77, no. 5 (February): 38–43.

Cherry-Paul, Sonia, and Dana Johansen. 2019. *Breathing New Life into Book Clubs: A Practical Guide for Teachers*. Portsmouth, NH: Heinemann.

Costa Arthur L., and Bena Kallick (eds.). 2008. *Learning and Leading with Habits of Mind: 16 Essential Characteristics for Success*. Alexandria, VA: ASCD.

Dorfman, Lynne, and Rose Cappelli. 2012. *Poetry Mentor Texts: Making Reading and Writing Connections, K-8*. Portland, ME: Stenhouse.

Dorfman, Lynne, and Diane Dougherty. 2017. *A Closer Look: Learning More about Our Writers with Formative Assessment*. Portland, ME: Stenhouse.

Fisher, D., and N. Frey. 2013. *Better Learning through Structured Teaching: A Framework for the Gradual Release of Responsibility*. 2nd ed. Alexandria, VA: ASCD.

Fleming, Nora. 2019. "Why Diverse Classroom Libraries Matter." *Edutopia*. https://www.edutopia.org/article/why-diverse-classroom-libraries-matter.

Fountas & Pinnell Literacy Blog. 2019. "What Are Reading Minilessons?" https://fpblog.fountasand pinnell.com/what-are-reading-minilessons.

Goodman, Yetta, and Gretchen Owocki. 2002. *Kidwatching: Documenting Children's Literacy Development*. Portsmouth, NH: Heinemann.

Goudvis, Anne, Stephanie Harvey, and Brad Buhrow. 2019. *Inquiry Illuminated: Researcher's Workshop across the Curriculum*. Portsmouth, NH: Heinemann.

Harvey, Stephanie, and Harvey Daniels. 2009. *Comprehension and Collaboration: Inquiry Circles in Action*. Portsmouth, NH: Heinemann.

Harvey, Stephanie, and Ann Goudvis. 2000. *Strategies That Work*. Portland, ME: Stenhouse.

Hattie, J. (2009). *Visible Learning: A Synthesis of Over 800 Meta-analyses Relating to Achievement*. London: Routledge.

References

International Literacy Association. 2018. Literacy Leadership Brief, *The Power and Promise of Read-Alouds and Independent Reading*.

Jenkins, Carol Brennan. 1999. *The Allure of Authors: Author Studies in the Elementary Classroom*. Portsmouth, NH: Heinemann.

Johnston, Peter H. 2004. *Choice Words: How Our Language Affects Children's Learning*. Portland, ME: Stenhouse.

Johnston, Peter H. 2012. *Opening Minds: Using Language to Change Lives*. Portland, ME: Stenhouse.

Johnston, Peter H. 2013. Reading Recovery Conference of North America. Columbus, Ohio.

Keene, Ellin Oliver, and Susan Zimmerman. 1997. *Mosaic of Thought: Teaching Comprehension in a Reader's Workshop*. Portsmouth, NH: Heinemann.

Kittle, Penny. 2012. *Book Love: Developing Depth, Stamina, and Passion in Adolescent Readers*. Portsmouth, NH: Heinemann.

Krashen, Stephen. 2004. *The Power of Reading: Insights from the Research*. 2nd ed. Portsmouth, NH: Heinemann.

Laminack, Lester. 2019. "Read Aloud Experiences Are Essential in the Development of Readers and Writers." http://www.lesterlaminack.com/blog/posts/23969.

Landrigan, Clare, and Tammy Mulligan. 2013. *Assessment in Perspective: Focusing on the Reader behind the Numbers*. Portland, ME: Stenhouse.

Landrigan, Clare, and Tammy Mulligan. 2018. *It's All about the Books: How to Create Bookrooms and Classroom Libraries That Inspire Readers*. Portsmouth, NH: Heinemann.

Layne, Steven L. 2015. *In Defense of Read Alouds: Sustaining Best Practice*. Portland, ME: Stenhouse.

Miller, Debbie. 2008. *Teaching with Intention: Defining Beliefs, Aligning Practice, Taking Action, K–5*. Portland, ME: Stenhouse Publishers.

Miller, Debbie. 2018. *What's the Best That Could Happen? New Possibilities for Teachers and Readers*. Portsmouth, NH: Heinemann.

Miller, Debbie, and Barbara Moss. 2013. *No More Independent Reading Without Support*. Portsmouth, NH: Heinemann.

References

Miller, Donalyn, with Susan Kelley. 2014. *Reading in the Wild: The Book Whisperer's Keys to Cultivating Lifelong Reading Habits*. San Francisco, CA: Jossey-Bass.

Miller, Donalyn, and Colby Sharp. 2018. *Game Changer! Book Access for All Kids*. New York: Scholastic.

Newkirk, Thomas. 2009. *Holding On to Good Ideas in a Time of Bad Ones: Six Literacy Principles Worth Fighting For*. Portsmouth, NH: Heinemann.

National Council of Teachers of English. 2013. "Formative Assessment that Truly Informs Instruction" (position statement). https://secure.ncte.org/library/NCTEFiles/Resources/Positions/formative-assessment_single.pdf?_ga=2.2371509.462823253.1593782935-910307521.1563463360.

Pearson, P. David, and Margaret C. Gallagher. 1983. "The Instruction of Reading Comprehension." *Contemporary Educational Psychology* 8(3): 317–344.

Rami, Meenoo. 2014. *Thrive: Five Ways to (Re)Invigorate your Teaching*. Portsmouth, NH: Heinemann.

Robb, Laura. 1998. *Easy-to-Manage Reading and Writing Conferences*. New York: Scholastic.

Rosenblatt, Louise M. 1978. *The Reader, the Text, the Poem: The Transactional Theory of the Literary Work*. Carbondale: Southern Illinois University Press.

Rosenblatt, Louise M. 1982. "The Literary Transaction: Evocation and Response." *Theory into Practice* 21: 268–277.

Routman, Regie. 2018. *Literacy Essentials: Engagement, Excellence, and Equity for All Learners*. Portland, ME: Stenhouse.

Routman, Regie. 2003. *Reading Essentials: The Specifics You Need to Teach Reading Well*. Portsmouth, NH: Heinemann.

Serafini, Frank. 2006. *Around the Reading Workshop in 180 Days*. Portsmouth, NH: Heinemann.

Serravallo, Jennifer. 2010. *Teaching Reading in Small Groups: Differentiated Instruction for Building Strategic, Independent Readers*. Portsmouth, NH: Heinemann.

References

Serravallo, Jennifer. 2015. *The Reading Strategies Book: Your Everything Guide to Developing Skilled Readers*. Portsmouth, NH: Heinemann.

Serravallo, Jennifer. 2018. *Understanding Texts and Readers: Responsive Comprehension Instruction with Leveled Texts*. Portsmouth, NH: Heinemann.

Shubitz, Stacey, and Lynne Dorfman. 2019. *Welcome to Writing Workshop: Engaging Today's Students with a Model That Works*. Portsmouth, NH: Stenhouse.

Smith, Frank. 1988. *Joining the Literacy Club*. Portsmouth, NH: Heinemann.

Stead, Tony. 2008. *Good Choice! Supporting Independent Reading and Response K-6*. Portland, ME: Stenhouse.

Szymusiak, Karen, Franki Sibberson, and Lisa Koch. 2008. *Beyond Leveled Books: Supporting Early and Transitional Readers in Grades K–5*. Portland, ME: Stenhouse.

Tovani, Cris. 2000. *I Read It, But I Don't Get It*. Portland, ME: Stenhouse.

Tovani, Cris. 2011. *So What Do They Really Know? Assessment That Informs Teaching and Learning*. Portland, ME: Stenhouse.

Turner, Julianne, and Scott G. Paris. 1995. "How Literacy Tasks Influence Children's Motivation for Literacy." *Reading Teacher* 48: 662–673.

Varlas, Laura. 2018. "Why Every Class Needs Read Alouds." ASCD 60, no. 1. https://www.ascd.org/el/articles/why-every-class-needs-read-alouds.

Vygotsky, Lev. 1978. *Mind in Society: The Development of Higher Psychological Processes*. Cambridge, MA: Harvard University Press.

Webb, Sandra, Dixie Massey, Melinda Goggans, and Kelly Flajole. 2019. "Thirty-Five Years of the Gradual Release of Responsibility: Scaffolding toward Complex and Responsive Teaching." *The Reading Teacher* 73, no. 1: 75-83.

Wilhelm, Jeffrey D. 2001. *Improving Comprehension with Think-Aloud Strategies*. New York: Scholastic Professional Books.

Williams, Lunetta M., and Libby McDaniel. 2017. "Peer-Recommended Books: Conduits to Increase Reading Volume." *Kappa Delta Pi Record* 53, no. 2: 76–79. https://doi.org/10.1080/00228958.2017.1299546.

Alexander, Kwame. 2019. *The Undefeated*. New York: Houghton Mifflin Harcourt.

Angleberger, Tom. 2010. *Origami Yoda* series. New York: Amulet Books.

Applegate, Katherine. 2017. *Wishtree*. New York: Feiwel & Friends.

Arnosky, Jim. 2002. *All About Frogs*. New York: Scholastic Reference.

Barnes, Derrick. 2017. *Crown: An Ode to the Fresh Cut*. Chicago: Bolden Books.

Barton, Chris. 2016. *Whoosh! Lonnie Johnson's Super-Soaking Stream of Inventions*. Watertown, MA: Charlesbridge.

Bell, CeCe. 2014. *El Deafo*. New York: Harry N. Abrams.

Bryant, Jen. 2019. *Feed Your Mind: A Story of August Wilson*. New York: Harry N. Abrams.

Byars, Betsy, Betsy Duffey, and Laurie Myers. 2004. *The SOS File*. New York: Henry Holt.

Byers, Grace. 2018. *I Am Enough*. New York: Balzer & Bray.

Casey, Susan. 2018. *Dolphins: Voices in the Ocean*. New York: Delacorte Press.

Coelho, Joseph. 2020. *Poems Aloud*. London: Wide Eyed Editions.

Duster, Michelle. 2022. *Ida B. Wells, Voice of Truth: Educator, Feminist, and Anti-Lynching Civil Rights Leader*. New York: Henry Holt & Company.

Erickson, Russell E. 1989. *Warton and the King of the Skies*. Boston: Houghton Mifflin.

Faruqi, Saadia. 2018. *Meet Yasmin!* (The Yasmin series—Early Reader Chapter Books). North Mankato, MN: Picture Window Books, a Capstone Imprint.

Florence, Debbi Michiko. 2015. *Jasmine Toguchi* (series). New York: Farrar, Straus and Giroux.

Giovanni, Nikki. (ed.). 2008. *Hip Hop Speaks to Children: A Celebration of Poetry with a Beat*. 2008. Milford, CT: Sourcebooks Inc.

Gravel, Elise. 2019. *What Is a Refugee?* Toronto: Schwartz & Wade.

Hood, Susan. 2016. *Ada's Violin: The Story of the Recycled Orchestra of Paraguay*. New York: Simon and Schuster Books for Young Readers.

Joy, Angela. 2020. *Black Is a Rainbow Color*. New York: Roaring Brook Press.

Kerascoet. 2018. *I Walk with Vanessa: A Story About a Simple Act of Kindness*. Toronto: Schwartz & Wade.

Lamba, Marie, and Baldev Lamba. 2017. *Green Green: A Community Gardening Story*. New York: Farrar, Straus, & Giroux.

Le, Minh. 2018. *Drawn Together*. New York: Little, Brown Books for Young Readers.

Lyons, Kelly Starling. 2019. *Going Down Home with Daddy*. Atlanta: Peachtree Publishing Company.

Lyons, Kelly Starling. 2020. *Dream Builder: The Story of Architect Philip Freelon*. New York: Lee & Low Books.

Maillard, Kevin Noble. 2019. *Fry Bread: A Native American Family Story*. New York: Roaring Brook Press/Macmillan.

Martin, Ann M., and Laura Goodwin. 2003. *The Doll People*. New York: Little, Brown Books for Young Readers.

Martinez-Neal, Juana. 2018. *Alma and How She Got Her Name*. Somerville, MA: Candlewick.

Medina, Meg. 2017. *Mango, Abuela, and Me*. Somerville, MA: Candlewick.

Medina, Meg. 2018. *Merci Suárez Changes Gears*. Somerville, MA: Candlewick.

Messner, Kate. 2015. *How to Read a Story*. San Francisco: Chronicle Books.

Murphy, Frank. 2019. *A Boy Like You*. Ann Arbor, MI: Sleeping Bear Press.

Murphy, Frank, and Charnaie Gordon. 2021. *A Friend Like You*. Ann Arbor, MI: Sleeping Bear Press.

Peete, Holly Robinson, and Ryan Elizabeth Peete. 2010. *My Bother Charlie*. New York: Scholastic.

Penfold, Alexander. 2018. *All Are Welcome*. New York: Knopf Books for Young Readers.

Pennypacker, Sara. 2019. *Pax*. New York: Balzer & Bray.

Pham, LeUyen. 2021. *Outside, Inside*. New York: Roaring Brook Press.

Reynolds, Peter. 2020. *Be You!* London, UK: Orchard Books.

Rockwell, Thomas. 2019. *How to Eat Fried Worms*. Reprint ed. New York: Scholastic.

Sotomayor, Sonia. 2019. *Just Ask! Be Different, Be Brave, Be You*. New York: Philomel Books.

Children's Literature Cited

Thompkins-Bigelow, Jamilah. 2020. *Your Name Is a Song*. Seattle: The Innovation Press.

Un Kim, Joung, and Soyung Pak. 2003. *Sumi's First Day of School Ever*. New York: Viking Books for Young Readers.

Venkatraman, Padma. 2020. *The Bridge Home*. New York: Nancy Paulsen Books.

Weeks, Sarah, and Gita Varadarajan. 2016. *Save Me a Seat*. New York: Scholastic.

Woodson, Jacqueline. 2001. *The Other Side*. New York: G.P. Putnam's Sons Books for Young Readers.

Woodson, Jacqueline. 2018. *The Day You Begin*. New York: Nancy Paulsen Books.

Yuksel, M. O. 2022. *One Wish: Fatima al-Fihri and the World's Oldest University*. New York: HarperCollins.

Index

Index

Index

Index

Index

Index

Index

Index

Index

Index

 *Index*

Z

Also by
LYNNE R. DORFMAN

Welcome to
WRITING WORKSHOP
ENGAGING TODAY'S STUDENTS WITH A MODEL THAT WORKS

FOR GRADES K–6

STACEY SHUBITZ & LYNNE R. DORFMAN
Foreword by Kate Roberts and Maggie Beattie Roberts

" If you're looking for ways to infuse new life into your writing workshop or a lifeline to get started, *Welcome to Writing Workshop* is for you. Stacey and Lynne share practical, quick, and doable ways to make the research-based writing process work in your classroom."

— **JEFF ANDERSON**
author of *Patterns of Power: Inviting Young Writers into the Conventions of Language, Grades 1-5*

For more information or to order,
visit Stenhouse.com

Stenhouse
PUBLISHERS